the TRUTH about you

By Ralph T. Mattson
  Mr. Slef (with Steve Hawley)
  The Truth About You (with Arthur F. Miller)

the TRUTH about you

Discover what you should be doing with your life

Arthur F. Miller
and
Ralph T. Mattson

Fleming H. Revell Company
Old Tappan, New Jersey

Library of Congress Cataloging in Publication Data

Miller, Arthur F.
    The truth about you.

    1. Success. 2. Self-perception. 3. Psy-
chology, Religious. I. Mattson, Ralph, joint
author. II. Title.
BF637.S8M55   158'.1   77-24446
ISBN 0-8007-0887-3

To those rare souls who saw the
vision and gave a helping hand

Contents

Part V: Permanent Principles

Part VI: Getting Down to Basics

Part VII: Benefits and Applications

Introduction

It is a curious thing to be a person. No matter how difficult circumstances may become, there are not many people who actually wish they had never been born. Most people cling to life with a great deal of tenacity and are willing to embark on marriages, spend many years in school, and invest nearly half a century in some vocation—all on the gamble that it will all somehow turn out to be fulfilling.

Gamble it is, for in our experience of counseling many hundreds of people of all ages and from widely varying backgrounds, we have discovered that a surprising number of people are in situations that can be described as unfulfilling or joyless.

Most people wish they could do something other than what they *are* doing. Many people feel they are nobodies and almost desperately want to be somebodies—with a calling to fulfill and a reasonable chance of pulling it off.

There are thousands of young people who are accused of not having direction in their lives, and most of them want direction but do not know how to find it. There are tens of thousands of adults who want some sense of purpose in their workaday lives, but who have little knowledge of how to go about getting it. There are hundreds of thousands of people who spend their lives as if they were adrift—trapped in their circumstances. There are millions of housewives, students, salesmen, bosses, waitresses, executives, ministers, and auto mechanics who do not fit the lives they lead.

Most people are uncertain about the rightness and usefulness of their lives. They are looking for signposts that will give them purpose and direction.

In this book, a process is described which can change the life of any reader who is unsure of his direction. It provides a practical way to discover the "why?" of an unfulfilling career and enable sound decisions about the future. In short, it can give you a practical perspective and understanding about the large and small affairs of life, moving a person from struggling in the sand to standing surefooted on the rock.

It is no longer necessary to gamble so largely about how to move in life. Though we cannot live without risks, it is possible to engage the future much more knowledgeable about what makes good sense for us.

There is a history in all men's lives,
Figuring the nature of the times deceased:
The which observed, a man may prophesy,
With a near aim, of the main chance of things,
As yet not come to life; which in their seeds,
And weak beginnings, lie intreasured.

WILLIAM SHAKESPEARE

Acknowledgments

In 1958, I was asked by the American Management Association to chair a week-long seminar on self-development. While gathering resources for this seminar, I encountered the work of Bernard Haldane, America's senior statesman in the field of career counseling. His work is referred to or copied without credit in almost every significant book or article I have seen on the subject of successful job finding.

Since those days when we worked together, I have pursued the more foundational implications of Mr. Haldane's "success factor." I dug deeply, documented carefully, began an achievement-interviewing process which at one point reached three or more hours, spent hundreds of hours sifting through achievements, and slowly began the series of discoveries described in this book.

A debt of gratitude is due William McConnell for his early financial and spiritual support of our work. In fact, it was he who named "motivated abilities."

Ralph Mattson early encouraged our work and began his own experimentation with staff and students in the educational field. In joining as coauthors, we trust this book is thereby more full of readable, useful, gracious truth.

I would especially like to express my gratitude to Carolyn Mattson for her patience and skill in participating in our work over many years.

ARTHUR F. MILLER, JR.
PEOPLE MANAGEMENT INC.
10 STATION STREET
SIMSBURY, CT. 06070

Part I

The Astounding Phenomenon

1—You Already Are

Who are you created to be?

The question is simple but, in today's world, quite revolutionary, because it suggests that the answer resides in *you* rather than in what your family expects you to be or . . .

What your boss is trying to make you
What your husband or wife wants you to be
What your teacher is telling you to strive for
What your friends are hoping you will accomplish
What society is trying to make you become

The world, for the most part, assumes you are something to be molded or manipulated or shaped or trained or taught—that you are the raw material for someone else's intentions. Our contention is that you have a design of your own—God's blueprint—and can only be fulfilled when you carry out that design, regardless of how high or low on the ladder of success you are.

Some people appear to have a destiny. From their earliest years, they seem to fulfill a design for their lives, whether it is inventing, composing, making money, painting, or politicking. Seeds of their eventual greatness were displayed so early that when fame came, the destiny seemed so obvious, the design so clear.

The idea of having a destiny, romantic and attractive as it is, seems reserved only for the famous. However, what is true of the great ones is also true of you. You also have been designed. You also possess what is God-given.

Probably like you, we had been brought up with the idea that we could become anything we wanted. Being Americans, we thought from our earliest years that all options were open to us if we were willing to work hard enough. We could become doctors or potters or lawyers or teachers or carpenters or actors or artists or plumbers—whatever we wanted. All we had to have was some talent to develop. In some cases, if we were willing to practice hard enough, we might even develop the talents we otherwise did not possess.

Then we encountered evidence that said otherwise. We discovered that people could *not* become anything they wanted. They could only become what was in harmony with who they were designed to be.

The technique we used involved a review of autobiographical achievements, extending from early childhood to the time of the individual's recollection. We discovered that a pattern of voluntary behavior emerged early in the life of every person we evaluated. More than that, we could see that the pattern remained consistent throughout the individual's life. Relationships and results which were fulfilling for the person as a child were fulfilling as an adult, though on a higher level of maturity.

Increased experience, additional education, and maturing processes of all kinds only served when they enabled the individual to fulfill, in one way or another, what he or she always wanted to fulfill. *In over three thousand cases, there was not one exception!* This was extraordinary, in view of the stance most of the social scientists and educators have taken. It not only went against the grain of much of our own education, but it presumed an understanding that denied the validity of man's corporate, institutional, and government procedures in dealing with people.

For example, *corporations* believe it is possible to train people to become what is needed—a manager, a salesperson, or a planner. We have a mountain of evidence to demonstrate that only certain people are managers (or salespersons or planners), and that no person with whom we have dealt ever "became" a manager or anything else fundamentally different from what he already was.

Schools believe that pupils who work for grades can be changed to become students who learn for learning's sake. We have discovered that this is not possible. *Churches* believe that pastors who may preach well, but who cannot administrate, can be encouraged to develop eventually into administrators. We have clear proof that it can never happen. *Mothers* who are motivated to make money and not raise children will not, in spite of years of actually raising children, become motivated to raise children. *Students* who are excited only about technological specifics will never, despite extensive exposure to the liberal arts, be converted to an enthusiasm for philosophic abstraction. *Scientists* who enjoy the craft of acquiring knowledge cannot be made to enjoy the craft of producing hardware, merely by paying them more.

People begin with a specific design that remains consistent through life and that design cannot be changed! This is not to say that there cannot be alterations in a person's life, since there are areas in people which need development or modification. Character requires molding and shaping so that *who we are* is worthwhile. Skills need to be taught so we may increase our effectiveness. Discipline may be needed to reshape sloppy work habits or life-style.

All of these improvements, however, enhance who we are but do not change our basic selves. Who we start out to be, as a child, matures, grows, increases in understanding and power, but the person to whom all this happens remains the same. As astounding as this discovery was to us, there was no doubt as to the validity of this truth, after experiencing absolute consistency in case after case.

A Phenomenon, Not a Theory. It is important to understand that we are not proposing a new theory of behavior.

What we are describing is a phenomenon that is clearly demonstrable and does not emerge out of statistical studies or psychological experimentation. We have made no attempt to make evidence fit a theory, since we began with no theory.

The phenomenon we describe does not show "quite often," or even "frequently." It shows *always*. In the same way that people are sure to have noses, the nature of a human being is such that each is sure to have a design that emerges in childhood and stays consistent all his life.

How is such a thing possible? If the evidence is so strong, why hasn't it been known earlier? While there has been research developed by a number of people which also supports our position, there are several reasons why many others involved in "people research" have been slow in accepting its validity. We believe the philosophic predispositions of most professionals dealing with people have slowed the pursuit of such an idea.

First, if researchers believe that people are essentially putty to be shaped by social influences and training, it would not occur to them to consider the possibility of humans as already possessing a shape. It certainly would be an unnerving idea to those who are intent upon the planning and development of human beings according to the needs of society or a utopian ideal.

Second, if researchers believe people are merely evolved animals without a will, without unique individual and inherent differences, the reality of what we have discovered will not be examined. The assumption that the will is only a biochemical process has been foundational in most research into human behavior and has generated a methodology which cannot even get at the individual.

Third, we know that people rarely take the time to even attempt to consider their own design, much less develop the thorough in-depth evaluations that characterize our work. Thus, no other data has been available for the kind of conclusions we reached. In addition, few have the advantage of the long-term relationships peculiar to our work, allowing the opportunity to observe people working out decisions which result from the knowledge of their own design.

We have been in an ideal position to observe the curious phenomenon of *individual* human design. We have reacted to those observations with a considerable degree of delight, for they lead to the freedom that emerges when we realize we do not have to be in the dark about who we are—it is possible to discover our own design. We can give up guilt for not becoming the person someone else wants us to be, and we can then move confidently in ways that are fulfilling.

Parents can have a solid understanding of each offspring's design *before* they invest thousands of dollars for an undergraduate degree. People entering careers which will impact on the lives and values of others can be—and ought to be—sure of their design before they become teachers, preachers, policemen, psychologists, physicians, or social workers. Those whose qualifications of education and experience fall short of their ambitions can examine who they really are and look for positions which can realistically fulfill them. People near retirement can understand their design so they can evaluate the reality of their dreams and make decisions about future activities which they and their spouses can live with. Young people who are about to prepare for careers—chosen primarily through the influence of parents or others—can justifiably object to the manipulation with considerable supporting evidence. They can look for and find and focus on their own design.

When we use the word *design*, we mean more than a description of talents or abilities. Anybody can list at least one or two talents that he knows he has. That is nothing extraordinary. What we are intent upon is something more basic. We seek a description of the essential pattern that resides behind a person's talents and determines how and when they are used. We aim at knowing that fundamental part of us that needs to be fulfilled before we can believe our talents have value.

2—*Where to Look*

To discover his or her own design, a person does not need to go through psychological examination, self-administered or otherwise. We need not be caught up in attempts to deal with our hidden selves and conjecture about the reasons which might explain why we are the way we are.

An individual's unique design can be clearly described without getting at psychological makeup—or in spite of psychological encumbrances which may be present. Either of these usually requires a lengthy and expensive process that is simply not available to most people.

It is, therefore, fortunate that the information we are after and the methods described in this book are not psychological in nature. The information needed does not require clever extraction, special knowledge, or formalized education. You now have in your memory all the data needed for the process we are going to describe. The data is not deeply hidden and does not require murky introspection. As a matter of fact, in collecting the necessary data, we need only deal with positives and never with complicated mysteries or negatives.

Signs of your design appeared very early in your life. In childhood, you were involved with certain activities which now stick out in your memory without your knowing why they should emerge so easily—while memories of hundreds of other things you did have been almost totally lost. These early signs probably were quite simple but (very likely) are good indicators of a beginning pattern of action in your life.

Early Signs of a Design.   There are many manifestations of the fact that you were already seeking to express your own design as a child: winning all the marbles—organizing everything in sight—a knack for drawing—exploring the unknown—enlisting in causes—showmanship—an inclination to "go it alone"—a thirst for experimentation—manipulating things that move—entrepreneurship—raising and growing living things—copying detail—an attraction to group activity—improvisation.

If we were to go through your personal history, we could find a host of things which you did that were meaningful to you, although you might not be able to explain why. They may seem to be a collection of unrelated or perhaps relatively inconsequential happenings, but, in reality, they are not haphazard and are evidence of your essential design.

There is a problem, however. How do we separate the actions which express *who we are* from all the internal and external reactions which actually have little to do with the basic design? The influences of parents or peers, indigestion, emotional discomfort, spontaneous reactions, psychological factors, economic needs, job requirements, and survival itself—all have a great impact on what we do and why and how we do it.

How do we extract from this complexity only those actions expressive of who we really are? The answer to this question requires an understanding of the will.

The Will. Everything we do is determined by the will—the core of our being which affects our attitudes, physical capabilities, and intentions.

The will has a shape which is as unique from individual to individual as are people's physical characteristics. Though we are dealing with a spiritual reality of human nature, which obviously cannot be described visually, the will can be said to have a spiritual shape which manifests itself by its intentions. As each of us has a unique physical shape in the design of our body, so we each have a unique shape in the design of our will—and correspondingly a unique pattern in the way this design expresses itself.

People *do* things. The way a person does them, or what he or she actually intends to accomplish, is not haphazard. They are not a collection of accidental happenings, since they come from a particular will with a particular design. Therefore, we can say that there is consistency in what a person does, so much so that we can describe it by using the word *pattern*.

If we examine what a person freely wills to do, we will find imbedded in his actions a unique pattern expressive of the person's basic design. Actions in response to another's will (or mere reactions to environment or needs) complicate the ability to perceive patterns. We have discovered a simple method to avoid such complications: IN ORDER TO DISCOVER A PERSON'S PATTERN, EXAMINE ONLY THOSE ACTIONS WHICH HE OR SHE FEELS ARE ACCOMPLISHMENTS THAT RESULTED IN PERSONAL SATISFACTION.

You may do something to please someone else, to relieve psychological or emotional pressure, because you need to survive in a job, or for a variety of other reasons. But, in our experience, the accomplishments which can be examined in order to understand the unique way in which a particular individual is put together *always* have two basic elements:

- They are achievements which resulted in a feeling of satisfaction, regardless of what other people thought.
- They are achievements which the achiever felt were done well, regardless of their degree of significance in other people's eyes.

Let us look into this more carefully. Note that we use the word *achievements*, and not the word *successes*. There's a good reason why this is done. Not everyone has a series of successes to remember. Everyone cannot be chosen for a team, elected to office, win prizes, or win a job promotion. Everyone cannot win recognition and honor for what he does.

Yet, each of us can search our memories to recover things we have done which gave us a source of satisfaction at the time, which we felt good about, which made us feel proud of ourselves. Events of this type we classify as "achievements." All of us have them. Our achievement experiences may never have been noticed by anyone else. In fact, our achievements may never have been visible to anyone else. Such deeds may never have brought us any praise or recognition. Yet, years later, even the recalling of these events brings back some of the satisfaction we felt at the time we did them.

Later you will have the opportunity to recall some of your own enjoyable achievement experiences and see what marvelous things they can say about you and for you. Therein lies a pattern which can be enormously useful in making decisions, evaluating relationships, and discovering direction. We are calling that behavior pattern your Motivational Pattern. In doing so, we are recognizing both the primordial factors resident in the depths of the will where actions are first initiated, and also proposing the idea of a recurrent theme, a motif.

The word *pattern* conveys the idea of a model that determines the shape of emerging actions. This prototypal idea is seasoned with hints of an artistic design which can suggest the beauty that can reside in the human will, when it manifests its gifts.

By examining your achievement experiences as they stretch from as far back as you can remember and up to the present, the Motivational Pattern can be described in detail. Most people are unaware of the abundance of evidence immediately available to them in making sensible choices in life. Most people have not spent as much as five minutes to consider such evidence. It is a rich resource, if you know it is available—and a potential "tragedy," if you do not.

3—Conforming to Your Design

Your Motivational Pattern is highly dynamic. Since it is the essence of your will, basic to who you are, every part of your being is keyed to this pattern. Your work life is good if it accommodates your Motivational Pattern and bad if it does not. Your learning experiences, recreation, hobbies, social life, and community activities all reflect your pattern.

There are many reasons why you can be depressed, but a most common reason for irritation, anxiety, or frustration is when "life" blocks the use of your pattern. On the other hand, you experience joy, completeness, meaning, and satisfaction when your design is effectively exercised. There is an enormous price in dollars and health and dissatisfaction paid by people who are in positions or jobs or roles which do not allow them to use their gifts, to carry out their design.

Jobs.   We know at management levels that few people are employed in jobs well suited for them. Conservatively, one-third are poorly matched with their jobs.

Family.   The family is the stage for a large number of problems because of misfits of people and roles. Consider men who are motivated to be in charge, married to women who want to be Number One—women motivated to serve, married to loners—men motivated to prevail, married to women who seek to please others—men motivated to be "hands-on" managers, raising sons who are motivated to be highly independent of authority.

School.   The effects in school—because of the failure to understand the uniqueness of the individual and to use intelligently the knowledge of Motivational Patterns—are incalculable. There are people whose gifts need the discipline of college, yet who are not attending college. There are students not motivated to learn, yet who are nevertheless attending college or graduate school, as there are people who are not geared to be teachers, yet attending teachers colleges.

Pressure to Conform.   Beyond your school, your job, and your family is a lot of world. And that world is composed of all sorts of pressures for you to meet.

Throughout your life, you have been asked and will continue to be asked to conform to somebody else's image or to function in a way acceptable to others. If that demand accommodates your design, you and your immediate environment are together. If you are different from what others want you to be, you and that part of your world are out of sorts. Unless you understand your design well enough to move into a compatible activity, you may be on the verge of experiences which are very costly because they prevent you from being who you really are.

Take the Time to Find Out

You cannot expect society or your family or your employer or your school to find out the nature of your pattern in order to discover how to relate to you. They have not done so—you need to. You have paid dearly by not knowing. Much is to be gained by you, society, your family, and your employer if you will take the time to find out who you are created to be—to discover your gifts.

The gifts we possess are more than ample for any reasonable but fitting task. When such a gift is carefully nurtured, subjected to the discipline of an education or apprenticeship, and used in a responsible, loving way, the product is beautiful to behold.

The Beauty of a Gift Exercised

Have you ever paused to watch a waitress, well suited for her work, serve a table of hungry patrons? How marvelously she handles them in their impatience—how she anticipates their requests—how neat she looks—how efficiently she moves to encourage, to recommend a selection, to replace some burnt toast—how her eyes constantly return to her tables as she makes her rounds! Contrast her and her gifts with the more common restaurant experience of being served by people who do not have the gifts required. There is a large and obvious difference!

Can you recall a teacher who turned on a light for you? Remember how she would make such complicated things seem so simple—how she would seem really concerned about you—how she would joke and storm and then grow very serious, all in the same class—how eagerly you looked forward to her class! Contrast her gifts with the other 80 percent of your classes, taught by men or women whose gifts did not foster learning. What a difference, when the gifts fit the job!

People gifted at their work are a wonder to behold. A shoemaker manipulating a fine piece of leather, a mother alternately disciplining and consoling a child, a repairman tracking down the trouble, an internist diagnosing an illness, an errorless typist beating the deadline, a cabinetmaker fashioning physical beauty, an executive secretary handling difficult people without alienation, the singer who transports you into her special world, the writer who moves you to smiles and tears, the minister who exalts, the artist who inspires, the coach who animates, the comic who makes the sun shine at night, the deftness of the surgeon and the toolmaker and the dentist . . . .

You Can Be a Gifted Person

Each of us—YOU!—can be a so-called gifted person, as is any of the foregoing, if you identify the gifts you have been given, submit them to whatever training may be necessary, and then employ your gifts in work which requires them. These are good gifts and, if used in work appropriate for them, will yield you and those who employ you much material and personal reward.

No person has achieved success in any field of endeavor except through reliance on gifts. What is true of the individual is also true of the organization. No business or institution has built a successful service or product except as a direct result of some men and women using their God-given talents. What was successful can only remain successful through other men and women using gifts which have been given to them. If those gifts are not present, what was a success will fail. There is no "self-made" successful man or woman. There are only people smart enough or grateful enough to be good stewards of their gifts.

So whenever you have the opportunity of observing a successful family or a successful bank or manufacturing company or retail store, you can be sure that enterprise has at least one or more key people with good gifts, employed in work accommodating those gifts.

Can you imagine what your life would be like if you did

what we are recommending? Can you begin to imagine how the world would benefit if people were educated and employed on the basis that each person was gifted? Regardless of how old or young you are—how low on the totem pole you see yourself—how impoverished your education or upbringing—you have been given good gifts. You have been designed and have a role to play that will fulfill you and please others.

Discover your design!

Part II
Gathering Data

4—Satisfying Achievements

This is an age when people are offered a large number of techniques aimed at self-knowledge. Many of these have their roots in Eastern religions and tend to be steeped in the mystical. Others are based on theories one must hope are true, since their validity cannot always be demonstrated. Procedures are often complex; some impact only on the emotional life and are inoperative outside that. In Motivation Patterning, however, the technique is transparent and the results come from the ordinary achievements in an individual life, as well as from the extraordinary.

Since we are dealing with a phenomenon and not a theory, we need only point out what is demonstrated in the everyday lives of ordinary people. As it has shown in the lives of every one of the hundreds of people we have evaluated, so it will with you. You need not fear that you have no Motivational Pattern, that you have no gift. Having a pattern seems to be an absolute ingredient of being human.

Before you gather the data for discovering your own pattern, it will probably be helpful to examine some of the enjoyable achievements of someone else and see the evidence for that pattern. The case we present here is for that purpose. When looking over the achievements listed, you will see that they are experiences that begin in childhood and extend through adulthood. Remember, too, that each item included is justified by the satisfaction it produced.

The italicized words in each of the following sections were taken from a list of achievements written by the achiever. The words following are actual edited quotes from a taped interview which elaborated on how the achiever went about doing what she did.

Crows, Cows, and People

Childhood

Fixing up a crow's wing. Taking care of the bird for about a week and letting him go when he was well.

I guess I was seven or eight—I was always collecting animals. One day I walked into this crow—I guess it was a broken wing. I really wasn't sure—but it couldn't take off, so I carried it upstairs. Had a bird cage. Put the crow in there. So I took care of him. Then after about a week or so, we just opened the little door and let the bird find its wings . . . .

School Years

Working with my animals.

Had a cow, good old Elsie. She developed mastitis. Poor Elsie was a pretty good producer but not the best. My father wanted to sell her. I objected—I violently objected. She was one of my cows. I called the vet and he came out. He gave her some shots—made her a sack out of a rubber apron—hung it over her back. I worked with this cow three days straight. It stopped and never came back again—she became one of our best producers . . . .

Age 22–25

Became officer in U.S. Navy; received exceptional and outstanding fitness reports.

I took over a pretty much run-down education-and-information office and built it up to the point where everybody knew about it. When I walked in there it was a mess. Got rid of a couple of people—had them transferred out. Built up a library—wrote instructions as to what to expect people to do before they go up for their examinations . . . .

Age 26-30

Managed a singing group on "off-duty time." They won the District Talent Show and were sent to New York (lost up there).

Started talking over a radio station. Had my own program—base radio—had a program of classical music. Looked in the other room and there were four sailors harmonizing, so I started listening to them. They were not bad—they were going to sing someplace and then I found out they didn't make it because they got confused as to where it was. So I said, "You need a manager." We started out with the base club. About a year later we had covered fifty-five performances in the area—won the first prize in Charlotte. Then we got guitars organized and went up to Goshen—won there. The accomplishment there is organizing the kids . . . .

We can now point out that some of you were absorbed in the reading of the above lists of achievements, while others will have found it to be tedious. This, of course, is because your own Motivational Pattern is in operation, even in this exercise. We need not encourage some readers to examine such personal detail, since they are basically motivated to enjoy it.

The next step in developing insight into Motivation Patterning is to go over the case again, but this time attempt to add up common elements and determine the pattern. To help you do so, there are key questions you need to answer:

- How does she want to operate with others? (*By herself? With others? As the boss? How?*)
- What does she want to work with? (*Numbers? Things? People? Ideas? Words?*)
- What abilities recur? (*Evaluation? Persuasion? Writing? Studying? Organization?*)
- What is the thing she seems to get out of the achievements? (*Excelling? Building and developing? Acquiring things? Gaining a response?*)

Though the original material consisted of thirteen pages of achievements, you need only the material presented above, in order to reach some of the obvious conclusions. Check them against our findings:

- Motivated to be the boss—run things and people
- Motivated to work with people and groups (and animals)
- Motivated to work on needs and difficulties
- Motivated to work with shows and visible things
- Motivated to build and develop
- Motivated to persuade and advocate
- Motivated to control and direct others

Most importantly, the factor that is seen repeated in this woman's achievements is that her central motivation is to gain a response from others and influence their behavior. These facts are of fundamental importance in understanding how this woman should move in life. Alone, they are exceedingly useful. Together with the great amount of detail that was developed by us to support and enrich the basic facts of her Motivational Pattern, they become remarkably advantageous in planning career changes.

Now that you have had a taste of "enjoyable achievement" experiences and can identify some of the recurring ingredients of Motivational Patterns, we shall get you started in the fascinating experience of recalling your own satisfying achievements and seeing what they say about you.

5—Recalling the Joys

The first step in looking for your Motivational Pattern is to write down a number of things done in life which you enjoyed and believe that you did well. To assist you in that process, use the form in Appendix B, entitled "SIMA—Part One: Biographical Information."

In the process of recalling and writing down your enjoyable achievement experiences, you may find the following suggestions helpful.

1. Allow enough time to complete the form. On the average, counting thinking time, it takes four to six hours.

2. People have different styles of working. Use the style that is best for you.

(a) Some sit down and complete it all at once.

(b) Some mull it over—then fill out a little at a time.

(c) Some discuss it with others—then sit down to write.

3. Remember that you are not to put down just an enjoyable experience, but something you did, something you accomplished.

Not: "I toured Europe with my wife, and the Alps were beautiful."

Rather: "I fixed a grandfather's clock when I was twelve years old. It hadn't worked in two years."

4. Be specific. Try not to generalize.

Not: "I fix things around the house."

Rather: "I designed and built a three-decker birdhouse for a flock of swallows."

5. Be subjective. Tell how it felt to you. "The set design I made for the senior-class play really gave me a kick to do."

6. Write all you can remember about the part you played in the achievement. If it was part of a group effort and you did nothing different from the others, describe what all of you did.

7. Do not be modest. You are the key actor in every event. These are *your* achievements.

8. When you recall a significant event, write it down. Do not try to analyze or evaluate.

9. Write about the details of *what* you did and *how* you did it—the things that were central to performing the achievement.

10. Do not worry about whether or not you can recall that far back. You will remember something. Just make sure that you do not reject it because it seems silly, trivial, or unimportant.

11. Write what was important to *you*, not what was important to your family or friends. If some honor or recognition left you cold, leave it out.

12. The events may not come into your mind in time sequence. Do not worry about it. Get them down, no matter how they pop into your mind.

13. If you want more space, take it.

14. Let your achievements come out of any area of your life. They need not be limited to school or work experiences. They can come from family activities, the military, things you do in your leisure, and so on.

After you have completed your achievement listing, the second step is very critical to getting a detailed and accurate reading of your Motivational Pattern. *Using a tape recorder,* starting with the earliest of your achievements, read what you wrote on the form and then expand on the details. You should cover everything you can recall about the specifics of how you went about doing what you did. You should be able to talk for at least five minutes on each achievement. For example:

- Give *detailed examples* where you have referred in writing to generalizations—"I used to do a lot of 4-H projects" *or* "I made some very tough sales" *or* "I used to coordinate a lot of affairs."
- Give *details* of how you went about "organizing," "building," "persuading," "solving problems."
- Give *details* of exactly how you went about the process of doing something which can be done in a variety of ways, e.g., playing tennis, football, chess; sewing a dress; building a tree house; raising a cow; training a child.
- Give your *role* if it was a group activity, and explain what you did.
- When you finish describing an achievement, the way you function, in detail, should be obvious. If it is not, go after more detail to point out the *hows.*
- Try to cover how you got involved in the achievement activity.
- Describe in detail the objects you worked with. Perhaps you edited a school newspaper (or built a soap-box-derby car, nursed a patient back to health, decorated a room, or troubleshot a new product). Talk about each object in terms of its complexity, the level of your involvement with it, and any similar data which

would reveal insight into the nature of your talent and
how you move.

To help you in this process, study the following examples
from the descriptions by two achievers about how they went
about doing what they did. (Second part of each consists of
edited quotes.)

1. *Planted a patch of pickles; maintained, harvested, and sold the
crop—reinvesting part of the profits for several years in future
crops.*

When it came time to harvest, was taken to where they sorted the
pickles out. Got the checks back in my name—paid back for the
seed—put some of the money away. One-quarter acre—had to hoe
them and keep them clean. Had to be sure you pick them on time or
they get too big. Had to have a little judgment on when to pick them,
what size to pick. I really enjoyed the money and the fact that I was
making money—that I could produce something. Nice to look at the
field and see it nice and clean—fun to plant something and watch it
grow . . . .

2. *Writing, casting, directing, and starring in a senior-class
commencement-night skit.*

Remember more about that, I think, than anything else in
school—putting together a kind of takeoff on the last scene from
Hamlet where everybody gets killed. Enjoyed reading Shakespeare.
Wrote rhyming couplets—enough to fill in twenty minutes to half an
hour onstage. Got casting from people I knew in the class—got the
son of the principal. Directed rehearsals. Ran through the parts, got
them to memorize the roles, all without faculty assistance. It was the
hit of the particular occasion. My drama teacher insisted that I had
not written the thing. It gave me great pleasure—I enjoyed the performing aspect and the directing, putting it all together. Had many
aspects to it. It was a situation I felt a lot of confidence about. I knew
what I wanted to do. I was in the thick of it all—driving it, participating in it, getting some good reactions and vibrations . . . .

Documentation

Once you have talked it out, you have a gold mine of information on the tape from which you can work directly. However, if you have access to a good typist or someone who loves to write, collate what you originally wrote with what you said on the tape. You should end up with a number of pages of information about your achievements. This transcript will be used later when you develop your Motivational Pattern.

Part III
Preparing for Discovery

6—Five Major Ingredients

Having written and spoken about your enjoyable achievement experiences, you are ready to start looking for the Motivational Pattern revealed in your achievements. In order to do that, you need to know more about what you are going to be looking for. You need to know more about the five ingredients found in Motivational Patterns. They are present in every pattern, including yours.

1. There is *one motivational thrust* achieved—one central motivation of critical importance. Here are some dissimilar examples:

- Handicaps or difficulties were always overcome.
- Personal acceptance or response was always gained.
- Money was made or a material thing was acquired.
- The top position, the best role, or the fastest time was achieved.

2. There is a recurring *way of operating with others*. In their achievements, people reveal a characteristic way of relating to others. A few differing examples are:

- He was frequently put in the position of leader.
- She always operated pretty much on her own.

- She was consistently part of a team effort.
- He was concerned with influencing others.

3. There is a group of *abilities* present. Individuals show characteristic ways of getting things done. These include such abilities as:

- Writing reports
- Analyzing problems
- Designing a "widget"
- Negotiating and bargaining
- Teaching children

4. There is recurring *subject matter*. People get satisfaction over and over again by dealing with their favorite subject matter. Some examples:

- Figures are usually present.
- Money was frequently involved.
- A method was often developed.
- People were central to the achievements.

5. There are recurring *circumstances*. People find they are motivated when certain circumstances are present. Here are a few possibilities:

- Competition was frequently present.
- She was usually working to meet a need or serve a cause.
- His achievements frequently involved projects and programs.
- Results and goals are consistently mentioned.

In the next four chapters, each of the above parts will be developed in greater depth, in order to enrich your understanding as to how they function in your Motivational Pattern.

7—One Central Motivation

Every time you accomplished what you enjoyed and believed you did well, you achieved a result of great importance to you. You got something out of what you did. That "something" is always the same. No matter whether your achievements cover ten years or fifty years, are obviously similar in nature or apparently disparate, you consistently achieved the same *one motivational result*.

Every person has one result he seeks to obtain through his achievements. Once you discover what that objective is, you will find some clear evidence of it in every achievement recalled. Let us look at a few typical kinds of sought-after results. Your own *one motivational thrust* may well be included.

Acquire/Possess
Be in Charge/Command
Develop/Build/Structure
Discover/Learn
Excel/Be the Best
Gain Response/Gratitude
Gain Recognition/Honors
Improve/Do Better

Make the Grade/Fulfill
  Requirements
Master/Perfect
Overcome/Combat
Pioneer/Explore
Serve/Help
Shape/Influence/Control

The central motivations (one result) listed above are only typical examples and are not intended to be exhaustive. Let us look at several cases to show this dominant, repeating quality of the central motivation in a life, so you can see the kind of evidence you should look for in discovering your own motivational thrust.

Mr. Fix-it

In this case, we see a man who wants to make things work properly, to make things useful. That theme is the dominant force in his life. He approaches every situation in his life with that perspective and emphasis—"How can I make this thing work better or be more useful or effective?" Consider these examples from his achievements and in his heavily edited quotes see clear evidence of this central motivation:

Prepared pin mechanism on ream binder so that bundles would be tied. I was greatly satisfied to learn the tying mechanism, find the cause of the nontying and solve the problem in a simple fashion. Was completely satisfied—the fact that I found the solution to it and made it work . . . .

Completely disassembled a stopwatch and reassembled it after replacing the broken springs. The accomplishment was being able to put it back together and make it work . . . .

I derived satisfaction in being able to prove the structure quickly, in a simple way, by an approach that I thought of. What I liked about it was that I thought it up myself and that it worked . . . .

Discovered a reaction which gave useful chemicals. It was useful to other chemists in the group—they applied it in their work. Satisfaction—did give something useful . . . .

Look, Ma, No Hands!

Now let us look at the remarks of a person who wants to impress others, to gain a response from others, to have an impact on them.

Learning to read and write before going to grade school—it opened a lot of doors for me. Class clown—get up in front of a group of people and make them laugh . . . .

Played in the class play. Wasn't the lead role, but I got a fantastic ovation out of it . . . .

Spoke at a few dinners—was the M.C.—telling the jokes between the acts. Really fun to keep it alive.

Student-taught for a very tough critic teacher. I opened the door to hear him say, "He's got them eating right out of his hand." School wound up offering me a job. I got it from the kids, too, saying, "We thank you; glad you were my English teacher."

Had a summer job with a large steel company as a foreman. Was offered a job at the end of the summer because they liked my performance. Something about getting a job offer that makes me feel awfully good.

In spite of all the complex theories about motivations, their transient nature, their illusive quality—each person has one central, very special drive which dominates his voluntary work behavior. We each have a "hot button," an unsatisfiable object of our affections.

Just Get Me Started

We'll close this chapter with the case of a woman whose motivational thrust in life is to take what exists and decorate it, embellish it, elaborate on it in some way, make it more complete or beautiful, or adapt it for some different purpose. Look at excerpts from her achievements which support this conclusion.

My earliest remembrance is sewing buttons, rickrack and fringe on skirts made out of my little brother's diapers. Loved making things with my hands, like a rose, cross-stitched on a hand towel, crocheted purse, stuffed poodle, and potato-printed place mats . . . .

Loved dancing in the living room to records—just did what came to you . . . .

Baby-sitting job. One time at the beach, I had kids make sand sculptures—not just sand castles, but something that actually was a person.

Won a prize for flower arrangement—used flowers that were around. Just went outside, saw what was around . . . . I did a sculpture of a dancer—a pose I'd seen a lot in dance class. Put it into sculpture . . . .

In charge of two art programs. I saved things—had junk that I'd bring in. Being resourceful—kids used it up. Once we decorated my car with streamers and drove around the block . . . .

As in these three cases, so it has been for every one of the people we have evaluated. Each one has a primary thrust—

one central, very special drive which dominates his or her
voluntary behavior. It is actually his *gift*, which, if used
rightly, is of great benefit to himself (because it gives him joy)
and to others (because he will work well). When a person's
motivational gift is not used in a beneficial way, the results
have serious negative consequences, which we will explain in
a later chapter.

8—*Operating With People*

A second part of the Motivational Pattern is how you are
motivated to operate with others. When you examine your
enjoyable-achievement experiences, you will find that you
seek out a particular role or relationship with others. For
example, one person will consistently do things alone;
another will be part of a group or team; another person will
seek out the manager role; another will emerge as a coach or
advisor of others.

There are few more critical career and role questions than:
"Am I a manager or not?" It is possible to answer that question early in life, even well before the educational process has
been completed. If you look at your satisfying achievement
experiences, the answer will be clear. You do not have to try
and then fail, in order to realize that you have been climbing
the wrong ladder.

There are other questions answered by this area of the
Motivation Patterning. They are asked in every organization,
as well as in many families.

- Who runs this place, you or me?
- Why do we fight so much when we try to work together?
- Could she organize her part of town?
- Is she a one-boss secretary?
- Can he handle a project without line authority?
- People like her, but can she manage?

Answers to these and other similar questions are available by examining the achievement experiences of the persons involved and determining the nature of their desired relationships with others. People will be—or strive to be—what they are motivated to be. The answers are unmistakably clear.

Some of the typical ways in which people operate with one another are the following:

Team Member	Wants to be with one or more others
Individualist	Wants his role defined and to get results without having to rely on others
Team Leader	Can lead others, but wants also to be involved in the action
Director	Wants others to do things exactly the way he wants them to be done
Coordinator	Likes to be at the hub of the action and get a variety of others' efforts plugged in when needed
Coach	Wants to help others develop their talent or improve their knowledge
Manager	Wants to get results by managing the talents of others

A person may be just one of the foregoing (such as an *individualist*) or may be a combination of two (an *individualist* when operating alone and a *director* when with a group, where he uses people as an extension of his individualism).

In addition to the preceding, some people will exhibit a certain way of operating with the "authorities" in their lives. Some people will manifest a motivation to take a close, supportive relationship with their bosses, husbands, teachers, or pastors. Others will want their leaders to point them in a direction and then get out of the way. Others want to work only for people who are their equivalent. Each of these qualities can be noted when present and added to the understanding of the Motivational Pattern of that person.

Look at cases from our files which reveal different types of relationships. Here, as elsewhere in the process of identifying the Motivational Pattern, we have added up the words used by the achiever, to reach the conclusions shown by the headings. Note the italicized clues in the edited quotes.

"Togetherness"—A Team Member

We did something every waking hour. *We* used to skate and maneuver in all those people. Exploring new areas *with two or three friends*. Decide to let's go exploring. Built them *ourselves*—done in group. *My friends and I* used to fix things up. *We* all had bicycles. *We* built rafts—*my brother and I*. All pulled *together*.

Always kind of a *cooperative* thing—there was no leader—usually a *mutual* kind of thing. Bride and I *worked together* where it took two. Designed *our* own house—of course my wife *worked with me*.

One of *my friends and I* started small business. Talking with my boss, *we* got idea. Head editorial *committee*. Got friendly with lexicographer—*we worked together*. *Committee* to make determination of proper definitions—oftentimes *we* said, "No, that's not what that word means." Enjoyed *working with* the men who had gained prominence in my chosen field. I was *one of the team*—the *camaraderie* among us. *We* spent all afternoon discussing what *we* should do.

"Doing It Myself"—An Individualist

I learned to speak English—learned it *secretly*. *I* gave the best talk of the year in fourth grade. *I* "invented" solution to problem on test. Did a lot of studying *alone* in areas other than school assigned. Found *I* could win easily on either side of debating issue. *I beat the system*.

Steel mill having problem—everyone was standing around in a puzzled way. Popped into *my mind* that there was not sufficient water to permit acid to fully ionize. Said, "Why don't you add several hundred gallons of water?"

Asked to write "lead paper"—it allowed *me* to emphasize the *unconventional* areas *I* had. *I* was able to put it all together into this "healing" concept. I evolved curriculum, found teachers—administration gave *me* a building. *I* was jokingly referred to as the Dean.

With no help, I planned and erected a two-room addition to *my* house. Transferred—moved into new home and did all *my own fixing up*. Special gratification in having done it *myself*.

I was chosen *chairman* of intragovernment committee.

"Do It the Way I Want It"—A Director

Getting it the right size to fit the doll—trading with a friend so *I got the color I wanted*. Playing store—assembling jars, cans, pricing items, making sales, using cash register, making change.

Editing high-school paper—typing and mimeographic—*correcting* people's spelling, grammar. *Edited* college newspaper—really got your hands into the printer's ink. Messed around with the *production* part of it—*layout* and *making stories fit*. *Decide* what you're going to feature.

Learning to drive car—drive at speed where *I was in control* of the car.

I did well at *organizing* and keeping track of detail. Business office—a neat package—one you could easily encompass. *Get your hands on*—sort the mail. *Organize* things into piles.

Provide home atmosphere. I took *initiative* in inviting people. *Set the tone*—at a pleasant conversational level—at a nonaggressive, nonconfrontation level. *Decide* what activities and what results *you want*. *Plan menu* in advance. *Make arrangements* in advance—used millions of three-by-five file cards.

Manager

Hired and trained C—— S——; he made star salesman by the end of the year. *Took over* an office that was demoralized; *arranged* retirement for former manager. Took an interest in all staff—turned responsibility over to new assistant and *achieved new goals*. *Made a few people changes;* helped one manager get hold of himself. *Held* series of *management meetings*—developed *esprit de corps* so as to have a smooth-running division. Got all my managers together—*give them all the tools* they needed—get them convinced we were going to do it. *Got them educated* and motivated—followed up by regional sales meetings.

The foregoing cases indicate the varying, individual manner in which some people operate with others. Similarly, *you* have a characteristic role you play in relation to others—which you will be able to identify later on.

9—*Using Certain Abilities*

The third part of the Motivational Pattern contains the abilities a person is impelled to use—usually from five to seven in number. A person should recognize that he also has abilities that are outside his pattern, and if he is forced by circumstances to use these abilities, he may perform in an acceptable way, but at a level below his potential. He will not be motivated to use any abilities outside of his Motivational Pattern and will only excel in using abilities that are part of his pattern.

Identifying abilities merely requires that you add up certain words used by the achiever. A few examples of such abilities include:

Administer/Maintain
Analyze/Evaluate
Build/Develop
Control/Schedule
Convince/Persuade
Create/Shape
Design/Draw
Do/Execute
Formulate/Theorize
Innovate/Improvise
Learn/Study
Make Friends/Build
    Relations

Nurture/Nurse
Observe/Comprehend
Operate/Run
Organize
Perform/Entertain/Be a
    Showman
Plan
Practice/Perfect
Research/Experiment
Synthesize/Harmonize
Teach/Train
Write/Communicate

Each of us will seek to do those things we are motivated to do. A person who is motivated to teach others will do so (or strive to do so), regardless of whether or not that is what is needed. A person motivated to innovate will so strive, even though it is not wanted or needed. Someone motivated to "put the house in order" will do so, even though everybody else can see eight other priorities needing more attention. Each of us perceives what needs to be done in a way which allows us to do what we are motivated to accomplish.

We have taken three abilities from the list and provided evidence from the achievements of three different clients to support the conclusions. Again, italics provide clues to the Motivational Pattern.

The Ability to Build and Develop
(Structures, Living Things)

Bought feeders, poultry, and *raised* them completely—a thousand chickens, a hundred turkeys, a hundred ducks per year. *Built* all of the houses and pens; *set up* a brooder area for the young birds. *Building* my own rig, blinds, decoys . . . . *Developing* areas—*building* from the point of view of everyone in the office . . . . One thing I like to do is *garden*—started *raising* lettuce—*planting* a seed and seeing it *grow.*

The Ability to Convince and Persuade
(Anybody Around)

At ages five and six—being able to *read aloud. Ran convention* in fifth grade. Put on *demonstration* for student body—convinced myself I didn't have any problem *speaking* before large audience . . . . *Convincing* fellows they really could play ball. *Convince* them they ought to get together and practice. *Put pressure* on fellows who had athletic ability—sales job to try to *sell* the fraternity . . . . Had to come to Washington and *explain* to people running this why it was necessary—had to *convince* them. I had to *convince* some of the engineers to collect data . . . . I *convinced* them they ought to pull that model out. Get all these guys in a room—*talk to them.*

The Ability to Organize
(Anything in Sight)

Organized neighborhood kids. Put on a fair—*rounding up* kittens and rabbits—called the *organizer* . . . . *Setting up* filing systems . . . . Got a group of *people together. Organized* an investment club . . . . Bringing in speakers. *Bring it together.* Getting a group of *people together. Set up* a schedule . . . . One of four women who *organized* Columbus chapter of the national organization. *Organizing* the foods, church, clothing—get everything ready right down to the last . . . . Had to *redesign the layout. How* you file up to the food area—roped it off—people coming down center aisles and fanning out.

After reading the preceding examples, you should have a fair idea of what kinds of things to look for when you go over your own achievements, in order to discover the motivated abilities in your Motivational Pattern.

10—Subject Matter and Circumstances

The fourth and fifth parts of the Motivational Pattern concern the subject matter (people, ideas, things, or numbers) and the circumstances associated with the achievement (stress circumstances, problems, projects, or causes). Normally there would be three or four items under these parts of the Motivational Pattern for each individual.

Subject Matter

A few examples of typical *subject matter* are:

Art/Design	Money
Concepts/Ideas	People Relationships
Controls/Schedules/	Physical/Structural Things
Budgets	Systems/Methods
Details/Data	Technical (Mechanical
Graphics	or Chemical) Things
Hardware/Equipment	Words/Language/Symbols

Consider a salesperson of small motors whose subject matter includes *people relationships*—and not *money* or *hardware.* In his work, he will stress his relationships with customers and be well thought of by responsive customers. At best, he will be listless about profitability and product knowledge, and superficial when dealing with the *technical* aspects of his customers' needs.

Guess how the household chores will and should be divided when the wife is motivated to work with *details, budgets,* and *structural things,* and the husband is motivated to work with *words, people,* and *art.*

A scientist who is motivated to work with *concepts* and not *hardware* will do just that. The engineer motivated to work with *hardware* and not theories (*concepts*) or math (*details*) will function as a technician—which can work well, depending upon how he is used and what is expected from him.

The wife motivated to work with *people* and not *physical things* or *money* would likely be a marginal housekeeper and give her bank and her husband an abundance of money problems. The secretary motivated to work with *details* and not *people* would be strong on clerical activities and not the best at handling the "personal" side of her job.

Examine some examples of certain subject matter found in two individuals' achievement experiences. Italics indicate the clues. Later you will look to see what subject matter your own achievements reveal.

Hardware/Equipment

Dismantle *clock*. Making *scooters* out of orange crates. Wind-up *phonograph. Air conditioner* on my car . . . . Hudson automobile *engine*—tear the *engine* down—make measurements on all the parts . . . . All principal systems of *submarine:* power, propulsion, ballasting, trim, ventilation, heating . . . . Loosened *bolts—coupling* misaligned—went to *machine shop* for stock. Aligned *shafts* experimentally . . . . Troubleshooting on Navy *electronic equipment.* Built self-contained, completely controllable pulse *generator* to drive up to one hundred radars. Built dual-time code *decoder* and *buffer.*

Systems

Reorganized the college bookstore in *supermarket style. System* I developed is still being used today . . . . Salvaged a production-control *system* . . . . Coordinated the *longest land move* of Marine Division in Korea. . . . Developed a practical *system* for controlling manufacturing operations. *Organized* the PERT office. Developed the Cost Index *System.* Participated in symposium on management *systems.* Developed a *system* for following ADP work orders.

Circumstances

What is true of subject matter is true of *circumstances* or the context within which a person is motivated to operate. Here are a few examples:

Competition/Test   Projects/Programs
Constraints/Deadlines   Stress Circumstances
Enterprise/Business   Structural Situation
Growth Opportunity/Potential   Trouble/Difficulty/
Needs/Causes   Problems
New/Novel Situation

For example, the salesman, wife, accountant, or industrial engineer who is motivated to work on problems (*trouble*) will look for one to solve—or, if pressed enough by a time of serenity, will make up one to be solved. The person motivated to work on *projects* will projectize whatever lends itself to being handled in that way. The person turned on by *stress circumstances*—or *competition,* combat, adversity or trouble—will gravitate to that part of his work. The wife drawn to *needs* and *causes* will respond—yes, that's right—day and night and weekends.

You can believe that the person motivated to produce results through his general achievement experiences will do so in his current job. The engineer or housewife motivated to work within *constraints* or *deadlines* (time or dollars) will make such attainment a matter of highest personal priority.

As with other parts of the Motivational Pattern, the presence of one or another circumstance is determined by adding up words of reasonably similar meaning. Examine the following examples, each taken from one person's achievements. Note the italics.

Competition/Test

Liked to test *myself*—liked to take *tests*. Never avoided the opportunity of *testing* myself. . . . I like to get called in to help *solve a problem* . . . . Then it became a *detective game* to find out what had really happened . . . . Welcomed the opportunity in junior high school for athletic *competition*. One of the *competitions* that I invariably entered and enjoyed was spelling. I enjoyed the *competitive* debate . . . . I enjoyed the *competition*. Could relate a dozen instances in which I have been the focal point of some *critical activity* in which a lot hangs in the balance . . . . *Competitive* flying.

Needs/Causes

We *needed* the food. Greatest satisfaction was bringing home *food for the family*. Especially rewarding to be able to *do something for country*. Battled *the flood* of 1955—helped to resume production two days later. Enjoyed *getting people out to vote*. Worked to help *support my family*—managed my father's store while he was hospitalized. Satisfaction was having a nice home to *meet the needs* of my family. Gave me a great deal of satisfaction to develop a fabric which would give continuity of production, and this was a *sorely needed staple*.

Your achievement experiences will reveal certain subject matter which you are motivated to work with and certain circumstances that captivate you. Understanding this very dynamic part of your Motivational Pattern will be an additional key to a productive and fulfilling life.

Part IV
Discovering Your Pattern

11—Rules and Options

When one of our staff members, after a year of training, writes a formal Motivational Pattern Inventory Report, he will take eight to ten hours and produce a document of twenty-five to forty pages. Half of the report will deal with the pattern itself, and half with the achievement listing. Obviously, there is no way for us to turn you into such an expert overnight, even if you had the required talents.

So when we made a decision to bring the principles of Motivation Patterning to any individual who would spend the time to read this book, we had to come up with a practical way for the reader to discover his pattern. That pattern information should be essentially accurate and detailed enough for the person to make foundational decisions about the direction and content of his work, education, or domestic career.

Another important factor in deciding how deeply into our procedure we should take the reader was that we had to recognize the vast difference between readers, their Motivational Patterns, and their need or desire to discover their own patterns. For this reason, we have provided procedures of varying complexity which the reader can utilize to discover his motivational thrusts. You can select the one that fits your needs and disregard the others.

There are rules, however, that apply to all procedures and must be honored if there is to be integrity in the patterning process. Maintaining integrity will produce an accurate Motivational Pattern which can be depended upon in decision making.

Rules of Motivation Patterning

1. Add Up—Do Not Interpret

The first rule about Motivation Patterning is not to interpret the words used! Merely add up words and phrases which have identical or closely similar meaning. If there is any confusion about the meaning of the words, consult any commonly used dictionary. If you are tempted to interpret meaning because you have not revealed enough facts, develop more facts or forget the item—do not interpret.

2. Add Up—Do Not Extrapolate

The second rule is not to engage in any leaps of construction or implication. Because a person won a debate contest does not indicate that he is good at handling people, and because a person built up an organization does not mean that he is good at running it. Stay within the facts revealed. Do not extrapolate further. Just add up what is obviously present.

3. Add Up—Do Not Play Psychologist

The third rule about Motivation Patterning is that the evaluator should not play psychologist, even about himself. Do not be concerned (for the present purpose) with *why* something was done. Motivation Patterning does not concern itself with an individual's psychological makeup or problems. Just add up what would be obvious to reasonable lay people.

4. Add Up—Do Not Condemn

The fourth rule is that you are not permitted to judge. Whether or not a pattern reveals a "saint" is not relevant to the Motivation Patterning process. Unless you want to play games with yourself, just add up what is obvious.

5. Look for Lifelong Demonstration

The fifth rule requires a lifelong demonstration of an item before it can legitimately be added to a pattern. If an item is present in only part of a person's life, examine what is similar about it and other items present in other periods of his life.

For example, as a child, a person used to sing and act, but that apparently stopped when he entered the world of work. Upon closer examination, it is found in adult achievements that the person had spoken before national conferences. So the thread is *not* singing or acting, but the more general one of Performing/Speaking and Demonstrations/Shows/Performances.

Options

At this point, select one of the four methods which can be used in evaluating your achievements and thus determining your Motivational Pattern. Chapters 12–15 give increasingly thorough techniques of evaluation—with Chapter 15 providing the most comprehensive approach to Motivation Patterning. Whatever method you choose, be sure to follow the general rules outlined in the previous pages.

12—*Free-Recollection Method*

As we have already recommended, you will arrive at a clearer, more detailed Motivational Pattern if you have written your achievements and talked them out—and then reduced both the written and spoken words into a single transcript. An alternative to taping your monologue is to talk to a friend and let him or a third person take notes of what is said. (See *Appendix C* for tips on what notes to take.)

However, assuming that you have documented your enjoyable achievements, either by yourself or with someone else, see how many factors you can identify which frequently recur throughout your satisfying achievement experiences.

Do not concern yourself with the five ingredients of a Motivational Pattern as described in Chapters 6–10, but simply put down what threads you find recurring. Once you have exhausted your ability to see these threads, put the matter aside and then return to it a day or two later. At that time, make sure to go over all your achievements again before trying to add to the items or factors you can identify. The following thoughts may be helpful to you in this process:

1. Are *people* (individuals, groups, the needy, high-potential persons) or *things* mainly involved?

2. Following some rough sequence, trace what you have repeatedly done with the person(s) or thing(s)—or both, if both are present.

3. Do you pick up any recurring themes of dealing in matters that are *concrete* (tools, cars, structures)—or are they more *abstract* (ideas, causes, theories)?

4. Describe how your achievements reveal your function with people (e.g., loner, member of group, individual role, boss).

5. Repeat some words or phrases which you have used in describing your achievements that appear to capture the essence of what was really satisfying to you about what you did.

6. Try to find what recurringly precipitated or led up to your getting involved in the achievement.

13—Checklist Method

You have previously written about your enjoyable achievement experiences. Reread what you wrote. If you took the time to tape your spoken expansions of these achievements, listen to the tape again. Now, to the best of your recollection, respond to the following requests:

1. Check four to six *abilities* which recur in at least half of the achievements.

Administer/Maintain   Assemble/Make
Analyze/Evaluate   Build Relationships

Control/Schedule
Convince/Persuade
Coordinate/Act as Liaison
Counsel/Advise
Create/Shape
Design/Draw
Develop/Build
Do/Execute
Formulate/Theorize
Implement/Follow Up
Innovate/Improvise
Interview/Investigate
Learn/Study
Manipulate/Motivate

Observe/Comprehend
Operate/Run
Organize/Put Together
Perform/Entertain
Plan/Schedule
Practice/Perfect
Promote/Publish
Research/Experiment
Scheme/Strategize
Synthesize/Harmonize
Systematize/Proceduralize
Teach/Train/Speak
Write/Communicate

2. Name two or three types of *subject matter* which recur in many of the achievements.

Art/Design
Controls/Budgets/Schedules
Efficiency/Productivity
Enterprise/Business
Figures/Details
Graphics/Decoration
Ideas/Concepts
Living Things
Methods/Procedures
Money/Profits
Needs/Causes
New Things or Ideas

Organization/Group Activity
People Relationships
Physical/Structural Things
Policy/Strategy
Projects/Programs
Stress Circumstances
Systems
Technical (Mechanical
   or Chemical) Things/
   Hardware/Equipment
Words/Language/Symbols

3. Name two or three *circumstances* which recur in many of the achievements. (Note the overlap between some of the subject matter and circumstances.)

Competition/Test
Constraints/Deadlines
Enterprise/Business

Growth Opportunity/
   Potential
Methods/Procedures

Needs/Causes   Stress Circumstances
New/Novel Situation   Structural Situation
Organization/Group Activity   Trouble/Difficulty
Projects/Programs

4. Name one way of *operating with people* which recurs in those achievements where you were free to function with others as you desired.

Team Member   Coordinator
Individualist   Coach
Team Leader   Manager
Director

5. Name the *one result* which you recall as being consistently present.

Apply/Actualize/Realize   Make the Grade/Fulfill
Acquire/Possess   Expectations
Be in Charge/Command   Master/Perfect
Develop/Build   Organize/Operate
Discover/Learn   Overcome/Combat
Excel/Be the Best   Pioneer/Explore
Exploit/Achieve Potential   Serve/Help
Gain Response/Gratitude   Shape/Influence/Control
Gain Recognition   Stand Out/Be Key/Be Special
Improve/Do Better

14—Pattern Approximation

The following are the steps to be used in approximating a more comprehensive Motivational Pattern from a transcript of your achievements or from listening to the tape of your spoken elaboration and reviewing your written achievements. You will need to pass through the achievement data, either written or spoken, more than once.

A. Identifying Motivated Abilities

Step 1: Extract and write down all verbs that denote actions performed while you were doing each achievement. (See samples on page 50.)

Step 2: Group together the verbs which fall within the following *ability* categories, but try not to identify more than six or seven groupings. If you believe that you have more, determine the six or seven most central to what was important to you. Examples are given for each.

- Investigative Ability (interview, experiment)
- Learning Ability (observe, research, practice, study)
- Visualizing Ability (conceptualize, picture, dream)
- Evaluating Ability (analyze, assess, select)
- Formulating Ability (theorize, define)
- Planning Ability (design, lay out, schedule, strategize)
- Creating Ability (invent, improvise, innovate, paint)
- Organizing Ability (collect, synthesize, systematize)
- Developing Ability (improve, tinker, modify)
- Construction Ability (build, assemble, put together)
- Operating Ability (manage, administer, manipulate)
- Implementing Ability ("do" physically, follow up, execute)
- Counseling Ability (coach, advise)
- Supervising Ability ("honcho," coordinate, supervise, direct)
- Performing Ability (act, demonstrate, dance, speak)
- Teaching Ability (train, instruct, explain, demonstrate)
- Writing Ability (edit, advertise, manualize)
- Influencing Ability (convince, motivate, promote, negotiate)

B. Identifying Motivated Subject Matter and Circumstances

Step 1: From the achievement information, extract and write down the nouns that are related to the actions when you are doing each achievement. These nouns will describe the kinds of objects and mechanisms you are motivated to work with or upon. They will also describe the situations, circumstances, or context within which you are motivated to work.

Step 2: Assemble these nouns in groups which denote similar objects or circumstances, as illustrated by the samples below. (See also lists of *subject matter* and *circumstances* on pages 52, 54.)

- The *objects* you work with:

  Figures/Details   Projects/Programs
  Living Things   Technical Things/Hardware
  Physical/Structural   Words/Language/Symbols
      Things   People Relationships

- The *mechanisms* you work through:

  Art/Design   Ideas/Concepts
  Controls/Budgets/   Methods/Procedures
      Schedules   Policy/Strategy
  Enterprise/Business   Systems
  Graphics/Decoration   Theories/Formulas/Math

- The *circumstances* you work within:

  Competition/Challenge   New/Novel Situation
  Efficiency/Productivity   Organization/Group Activity
  Money/Profits   Stress/Trouble/Difficulty
  Needs/Causes

C. Identifying the Motivated Relation With Others

How you operate with others is determined by examining the active role you maintain when performing your achievements in relation to others who may be involved in the activity.

Step 1: Examine the achievements for statements which indicate the way you relate to other people.

Step 2: Extract phrases which describe the relationship.

Step 3: Study these phrases that identify relationships with others and find the best fit from the following descriptions:

Team Member — Must operate in company with others
Contribution merged with efforts of others

Individualist — Content to operate either with others or by himself
Wants role and contribution defined and traceable to his efforts
Wants to be able to secure results primarily through his own efforts

Participating Leader — Involved with subordinates in the act
Influences their actions by example or expertise
While leading, may still tend to be preoccupied with his personal tasks

Coordinator — Causes actions by others who are not required to report to him
Prefers to operate without hire-fire or confronting authority

Director — Directs the actions of others to perform exactly his way
Gets involved at the level of detail
Uses people as extensions of himself

Manager — Manages the talents of others to bring about a result
Normally allows others to determine what they will perform
May tend to delegate authority and responsibility while still maintaining overall control

Coach — Develops others' talents in support role
Does not normally participate in act
Does not focus on or control outcome or result

D. Identifying the Central Motivation—One Result

Step 1: Using the samples below, examine your achievements for a common thread that either matches one of these or can be expressed similarly. You will probably be able to find a key phrase in the language used, which essentially describes the one result you are attempting to reach.

Acquire / Possess — Money / Things / Status / People. Wants to have own baby, to own toys, bicycles, houses, furniture, family, and so on . . . .

Be in Charge /Command — Others /Things /Organization. Wants to be on top, in authority, in the saddle—where it can be determined how things will be done . . . .

Combat / Prevail — Over Adversaries /Evil /Opposing Philosophies. Wants to come against the bad guys, entrenched status quo, old technology . . . .

Develop /Build — Structures /Technical Things. Wants to make something where there was nothing . . . .

Excel /Be the Best Versus Others /Conventional Standards. Wants to be fastest, first, longest, earliest, or more complicated, better than others . . . .

Exploit / Achieve Potential — Situations / Markets / Things /People. Sees a silk purse, a giant talent, a hot product, or a promising market before the fact . . . .

Gain Response / Influence Behavior — From People / Through People. You want dogs, cats, people, and groups to react to your touch . . . .

Gain Recognition /Attention — From Peers /Public Authority. You want to wave at the cheering crowd, appear in the newspaper, be known, dance in the spotlight . . . .

Improve /Make Better — Self /Others /Work /Organizations. Make what is marginal, good; what is good, better; what makes a little money, make a lot of money . . . .

Make the Team /Grade — Established by Others or System. Gains access to the varsity, Eagle Scout rank, Silver Circle, Thirty-ninth Masonic Order, the country club, executive dining room . . . .

Meets Needs / Fulfill Expectations—Demanded / Needed / Inherent. Strives to meet specifications, shipping schedules, what the customer wants, what the boss has expressed . . . .

Make Work / Make Effective — Things / Systems / Operations. Fixes what is broken, changes what is out-of-date, redesigns what has been poorly conceived . . . .

Master / Perfect — Subject / Skill / Equipment / Objects. Goes after rough edges, complete domination of a technique, total control over the variables . . . .

Organize / Operate — Business / Team / Product Line. The entrepreneur, the beginner of new businesses . . . .

Overcome / Persevere — Obstacles / Handicaps / Unknown Odds. Goes after hungry tigers with a popgun, concave mountains with slippery boots . . . .

Pioneer / Explore—Technology / Cultures / Ideas. Presses through established lines, knowledge, boundaries . . . .

Serve / Help — People / Organizations / Causes. Carries the soup, ministers to the wounded, helps those in need . . . .

Shape / Influence — Material / Policy / People. Wants to leave a mark, to cause change, to impact . . . .

Assembling the Pattern Into Summary Form

You have now completed the process of approximating your Motivational Pattern. Using the various parts you have discovered, assemble the pattern into its summary form as shown below, writing your answers on a separate sheet of paper.

1. What *one result* did you accomplish?
2. What *abilities* did you use?
3. What was your *relation* with others?
4. What *subject matter and circumstances* do you usually work with?

15—The Fourth Level: SIMA

If you have the desire and pattern to try to accomplish the most accurate and detailed account of your design, you can attempt the procedure followed by our staff in using our System for Identifying Motivated Abilities (SIMA).

Step 1: Starting with a completed SIMA form, Part One (*Appendix B*), have someone conduct a two-hour taped interview of you, using the form entitled SIMA, Part Two: Interviewing Procedure, contained in *Appendix C*.

Step 2: Have a typist transcribe the taped interview, collating it with the written achievements, editing only what is clearly surplus, and leaving wide margins on both sides of the page.

Step 3: You are now prepared to begin identifying the various ingredients of the Motivational Pattern.

In the right-hand margin of each page of the transcript, note all references to *abilities* used, *subject matter* worked with, *circumstances* surrounding each achievement, and *relations* with others which are clearly manifested in the achievements.

Clues to identification of these ingredients are contained in the previous chapter on Pattern Approximation. Also reread Chapters 8–10 and note the various samples which evidence a particular item.

On the left-hand margin of each page, note points which reveal a more detailed understanding—for example: *how one learns* ("imitates others," "does thorough research," "seems to learn by doing"); *how one teaches* ("seems to teach by demonstration," "teaching only one-on-one," "gets involved with students"); or *how one manages* ("keeps close track of subordinate's work," "spends time on people problems," "is confronting in the face of delay").

There follows an example of a partial page of a transcript of achievements together with the desired notations in each margin.

go out and talk to people
appearance image
strategy plan
80% response

...until now it's been a very haphazard
thing in terms of what training we do
give them, how accepted they are into
the management circle - that looked
real interesting to me - said I'd enjoy
going out and talking to people - see
if I can get the rapport - thought about
even how I am going to dress - so I put
on some grubbies - I felt that I did
some planning - had to make all my calls,
set up each visit - found a place where
I could sit down with each guy - 80% of
the people I talked to I felt really responded and opened up and told me how
they felt - we had a couple of startling
answers - I put it in the report - he
was impressed with it and I gave it to
about 20 people in a meeting - some of
the things that came out of....

plan strategize talk
interview
write editorialize synthesize

Step 4: By now, you should be sufficiently familiar with the transcript that you can dive into the large question of what is the "one result" or central motivation which is so important to you. Refer to the material in Chapter 7 for examples.

Picking the most likely *result*, try to find clear and convincing evidence of its centrality in each and every achievement. The words used to support the conclusion reached should be so obvious and compelling that essentially any reasonable person would concur. Examples of such evidence supporting the one result reached are contained on pages 43–46.

When you have found your one result or central motivation, list on a piece of paper all the evidence from each and every achievement which supports your conclusion. Show it to a critical friend and ask him to affirm the soundness of your evidence gathering.

Step 5: Now go after each of the other elements of the Motivational Pattern. Gather the words which seem to describe an *ability, subject matter* or *circumstances,* and *relationships* and put them together. Try to condense each item into one, two, or—at most—three words. For example: persuade/argue; experiment/tinker; schedule; improvise/conceive ideas/ innovate; stress circumstances/combat/challenge; team leader; new/novel situations; people relationships.

Limit the number of *abilities* to seven, the number of *subject matter* and *circumstances* to four, *relationships* to one or a combination of two.

Step 6: Once you have identified the items in Step 5, go through the validation procedure described in Step 4. Gather clear evidence from the words used in describing your achievements and place the words under the item supported. See Chapter 7 for examples of such conclusions.

Step 7: Now take any recurring points noted on the left-hand margin and show them under the appropriate item as explained earlier. The purpose in doing this is to amplify and make more accurate how the person functions with respect to the *one result, ability, subject matter, circumstances,* and *relationship*. There follow two examples of such amplification drawn from these left-margin notations.

Study/Investigate/Perceive.   She is an avid reader and enjoys learning by studying up on something. She has a good memory and this, combined with an ability to take things in both aurally and visually, makes her quick to pick up what is going on in a situation. The ability to perceive ranges from close examination of documents, for example, to general observation of work processes. She will move out on her own initiative to investigate what interests her. Asking questions of people is not difficult for her, though that is usually not her first way of finding something out. She enjoys the challenge of learning on her own and teaching herself how to do something, though in technical and procedural matters, she would prefer taking a course.

Deadlines/Disciplines.   He enjoys working under disciplines that he has created for himself, as well as under those that are present in his job. He enjoys measuring up to a task that contains deadlines and cutoff points that create a test for his abilities. In fact, any kind of restriction or discipline that would provide a challenge for him would be fitting for his central motivation.

Step 8: There are vital aspects in each person's Motivational Pattern, as noted in the left-hand margin of the transcript in Step 3, that are not related to particular abilities, circumstances and subject matter, relationship, or the one main result. These are designated "commentary points," and are described in short paragraphs with a heading which captures the essence of each aspect. Here follows one such commentary point:

Likes to Prove Out His Own Ideas

He seems to find enormous satisfaction in seeing some of his hunches come true. He frequently starts a project with an idea, hunch, or a feeling that a particular approach is the right way to do it. Seeing his idea proved out, vindicated, or demonstrated as correct reinforces his desire to realize personal wishes and ideas.

Step 9: The last step is simply the bringing together of all previous items in a Motivational Pattern Inventory Report.

Part V
Permanent Principles

The conclusions described in the next several chapters about Motivational Patterns are the result of many years of working with the phenomena involved. Thousands of hours have been spent poring over achievement experiences, gathering threads, perceiving how they form the fabric of a pattern, discovering interrelationships between parts and how they act to reinforce and support. As a result, we are now in a position to discuss major characteristics of Motivational Patterns with the authority which comes from long study, observation, and documentation.

The distinctive qualities we describe here are striking because of their immense significance to people and organizations concerned with evaluating and influencing human behavior. Individuals also benefit, since they can proceed to identify and cultivate *who they are* without lusting after some other design or role.

16—Pattern Consistency

Once the Motivational Pattern of a person emerges, it remains consistent throughout the remainder of his life. There can be nothing of substance taken from or added to the pattern. There is no influence within the control of the individual or another person which can significantly alter the basic character and content of that pattern.

This conclusion is based on the fact that we have never seen a significant change in the pattern of any person among the hundreds with whom we have worked. No change—in spite of changes (frequently, drastic ones) in environment, circumstance, personal influences, authority, experiences, education, values, philosophy.

In spite of attempts to influence the achiever—by mother and father, peer groups, teachers, Sunday school, lovers, war, depression, prosperity, spouses, employers, community, psychoanalysts—we have seen no evidence that such attempts at influencing have any impact on the *fundamental* shape and nature of the achiever's Motivational Pattern.

We are not saying that these factors do not have impact on a person. They obviously do. They can influence the direction of a life, the quality of it, the values embraced, and probably the level and intensity of achievement. However, what we have found is that an overcomer will seek opportunities to overcome—whether he is a brain surgeon, a salesman, or a construction engineer. A woman motivated to acquire material things will continue to do so throughout her life—whether she chooses or is influenced to be a housewife, a barber, a lawyer, or the owner and operator of a business.

Here are illustrations from the achievement experiences of two people who demonstrate the fixed nature of the Motivational Pattern, particularly the "one result" achieved. Each was subject to the sorts of would-be influencers and conditioning agents alluded to before, yet the pattern emerged early in life and stayed constant. You should now be able to identify the recurring key elements.

An Entrepreneur From the Age of Eight

This case is an example of a consistent pattern of building and operating a business. Note how he operates—organizing, scheduling, and managing—and how he is taken up with sales, dollars, profits. His methods of using new ideas and structuring, utilizing, and expanding upon what is available reflect a pattern which appears throughout his life.

Childhood
Established an egg route which was run weekly. About eight years old.

Started with a little shed on the side of the garage—had a dozen chickens. That expanded to where we had a two-car garage and I cut a hole through it and wired off a section. Ended up with 175 chickens—sold the eggs from those. Established egg route. First profits I got involved with . . . .

Age 22–25
Full-time job while in graduate school.

When I started I was on a graduate assistantship—what I had was a full-time job—making $125 a month. What we did was establish for the first time the first successful swine-testing station. I was involved in the physical building—the structures, pouring the concrete, and so on. I was in charge of keeping all the records. I organized the task of getting the animals to the sale barn—that the proper information was available—that the sales catalogue was correct and printed and published. One of those times when it had to work—and it did. Still running today—enjoyed making it succeed . . . .

Age 36–40

Selling extra research capacity to others.

Organized a group which is now allowed to go outside the company and sell our services to actually become a profit center. Trying to use excess capacity we have available in central research. So I said, "Let's sell that extra capacity and try to direct it to those areas where we have that capacity." Working quite well—first time that research people have become involved in a profit-type center. Started selling services by word of mouth. Developed some of our own advertising. Go to professional meetings—I've done some displays at those things.

Mountains Are Made to Climb

In this case, note the consistent, fixed pattern of overcoming obstacles and opposition, making independent judgments, individualism, practicing and persevering, and evaluation of values and concepts. Again, the Motivational Pattern can be seen recurring in this woman's life, beginning in childhood and extending into her forties.

Childhood

I learned to ice-skate. I was really thrilled because, due to a physical handicap, I was told this was something I would never be able to do.

People were always saying, "You probably won't be able to do that—you're going to have to learn to live with that fact." It just made me angry that people thought I couldn't do it. I can remember how excited and thrilled I was—I had gone to the park every day and practiced and practiced after school. Finally one day I invited them to come and watch. They were amazed—it showed me that I could do it—that they weren't right. It was pretty much an individual thing. I didn't ask anybody to help me . . . .

Age 26–30

In one year I weathered three major personal misfortunes—the sudden death of my father, the discovery that my husband had an incurable illness, and a miscarriage. I found that I could absorb the blows and go on with my life.

I never had had any experience with death. I don't think of myself as a particularly strong person. I just found out that I could survive—learned a lot about myself in that period. I spent a lot of time thinking, "What is important to me? Where am I going?"

Age 35–40

After much work, my son, who was diagnosed as autistic and emotionally disturbed, is now a healthy, normal, lovable child.

My son as a baby was totally withdrawn, angry, and unresponsive. At about nineteen months, he was diagnosed as being autistic. I could not accept that—I knew something was wrong with him and had been pleading for help for him for over a year. We worked with psychologists, read books, talked to people, and worked with him. Now, three years later, he is completely normal. No one can believe what he once was—he is extremely loving and lovable.

17—Pattern Irresistibility

Although the several principles of Motivational Patterns overlap, each has some distinctive quality. The second principle is its irresistibility—it will be expressed somewhere in the person's life. The pattern is alive, active, seeking opportunity to be exercised. Using the Motivational Pattern is the essence of meaningful activity to the person, although only rarely is the person actively aware of its irresistible character.

People find opportunities to exercise their Motivational Pattern in spite of the aridity of their environment. Surroundings which cultivate achievements would probably assure more frequent and richer achievements. However, we have much evidence which indicates that people will achieve in spite of even repressive environments.

For example, the only-child farm boy—miles from the next farm—somehow, by himself, finds enough mechanical problems with equipment, strategy problems with predators, and management opportunities with the chicken-and-feed-and-egg business so that he will go off to high school with a decade of achievements marking him as a likely engineering executive. This will occur with his particular pattern, in spite of apparent paucity of opportunity, no particular encouragement, little reinforcement, and no apparent outside conditioning.

Each person has within him this dynamic, unique thing which seeks expression and which will emerge in spite of the meanness and sterility of the surroundings.

Triggering Circumstances

With some people there is a definite precedent circumstance which precipitates an achievement situation. For example, being asked to help, being thrust into a situation where they must sink or swim—or having laid on them certain requirements or expectations—are types of triggering acts which seem a condition precedent to some people being turned on.

However, even with many of these people, the pattern is so irresistible that they will actively seek out such requirements as a ladder to climb (whether in the army or the Masons), outside courses to take, a contest to enter. These conditions will place in front of them an expectation or requirement, which they will then meet and thus experience an achievement. People will actually seek out triggering circumstances, even though they are unable to experience achievement until required to perform.

The River Seeks an Outlet

Look at a lifetime of achievement experiences. There are some related to the person's work. Then, for five or ten years, all the achievements are nonwork-related. A few—really very few—people have such a personally rich career that they are consistently able to pour out their gifts into their work. On the other hand, large numbers sooner or later find that many achievements are taking place outside their work. As examples of the foregoing, let us cite these:

Here is a person who wants to build and who has spent the last ten years of his life building or helping to build a recreation room, a patio, an extension to his house, a cabin in the mountains, a new scout troop, an addition to the local hospital, and a stereo system. In the twenty years prior, he had built much for his employer, but was in a "maintaining" mode during the current decade.

Next is a woman whose achievements for the first fifteen years of her career came mainly out of nonwork activities—initiating, organizing, coordinating, and running a variety of community and church activities and functions—until her company caught on, promoted her, and enjoyed the benefits of her gifts.

If the person cannot pour it out on his job, he'll give it elsewhere. One must use the Motivational Pattern someplace. Its use is the essence of meaningful life. It is a river that flows in a particular direction and channel—and you cannot stop it or dam it for long.

18—Your Pattern Leads

If you are true to your Motivational Pattern, it will literally lead you into a career. A fascinating case study demonstrating this principle is contained in an article by Roscoe C. Born, writing in *The National Observer*, week ending August 3, 1974. Here he called to the attention of newspaper journalists their propensity to "rattle the cages." He pointed out that the profession tends to be self-righteous about its truth seeking, whereas the journalistic crusader was drawn to journalism in general, and specific issues and exposés in particular, because of the way the crusader is put together motivationally. Mr.

Born says it well:

> I have come to the belief that there lurks in the character of nearly every journalist a fundamental flaw. I now believe that this flaw is probably there in even the most honorable and decent journalists, even though some have managed to overcome it in the same way that decent and honorable men and women have learned, over the years, to suppress or mask some of their baser instincts.
>
> I suspect this flaw I am trying to describe is an inborn desire to "get" somebody, anybody; to publish a startling story that will rush in an indictment, will get somebody fired, will get some public official ousted from office or defeated for re-election. A reporter who takes the hide off somebody in print reaps immense rewards and satisfactions. His colleagues praise him. His editors praise him. His non-journalist friends suddenly are aware that he has done something remarkable, and they tell him about it. He may even win one of journalism's most famous awards. For it is a fact known to journalists everywhere, that if one hopes to win a big award for reporting, one must be able to show that his stories got results: someone indicted, someone fired, someone ousted, someone sued. That is the path to journalistic glory.
>
> If this *is* true, how does it come to be? Are we all so indoctrinated in journalism schools that we enter the field brain-washed? I don't suspect that for a moment. And I think it borders on lunacy to suggest that conspiring journalists get together and plot the downfall of this personage or that. No conspiracy is necessary. Journalists crave the thrill of the exposé almost intuitively, whether alone or in packs.
>
> I believe this may be an important factor that led most of us into journalism. It's not something we acquire *after* we become reporters. Rather, it may be that the seeds of this desire, nurtured in all of us, caused us to become reporters . . . .

What is true of the crusading journalist is true of every finger-pointer, regardless of the timeliness or effectiveness of the crusade.

Saints and Sinners

The zeal of people in pursuing an objective is traceable to Motivational Patterns, whether they be consumer advocates, crusading congressmen, environmental enthusiasts, or witch-hunters. A zealot may be seen as "saintly" or "demonic" by the cause which is espoused and how *you* identify with it. However, if one were to examine achievement experiences up to the current crusade, the truth will out, the zeal is traceable to the Motivational Pattern.

People who are good at and fond of aiding the stricken—helping the underdog, working with those in trouble, collectivizing for material help, opposing the established—may consider their purpose a lofty one, which it may be, but they are better off if they do not kid themselves about their motivation. Similarly, those who are dedicated to changing people or changing the system are dedicated precisely because they "feed themselves" through causing such changes.

The fact that frequently the crusader's pattern is to tear down, rather than build up, explains why so many institutions once torn down have to wait for a new person to come along before anything significant takes its place.

This principle of being led by our patterns into a field of work continues, if we are well advised, into the depths and details of our crafts, roles, performances—how we express what we have to express.

We encountered a splendid example of this principle of Motivational Patterns in *Painting Techniques of the Masters* by Hereward Lester Cooke. Addressing the student artist on the subjects of color, style, subject, and convictions, he advised as follows (italics are added):

[On Color] One thing you must do early in your career is to find out *what color harmonies come naturally to you.* No two painters have the same sense of color harmonies, and it is very important that you *find out where your instincts lie* . . . . The history of art proves that the great masters—with only a few exceptions—found and kept to a rather narrow color range during most of their active careers.

[On Style] One of the most difficult and important things you will ever have to do is to decide just what kind of a painter you want to be.

No two people react in the same way to the world around them . . . .
This is an invariable rule of art history; only when a painter is painting what appeals to him, *in a way that appeals to him,* is there a
chance of producing a worthwhile picture.

[On Subject] Next, decide what subject *you would really like to paint*
if you had a free choice. Some people are *naturally drawn* to landscapes, others to flowers, abstract shapes, birds, machines, portraits,
nudes; the range of subjects is almost infinite. Again, *be honest with
yourself*. You will never be able to alter your *instinctive preferences*
. . . . For an artist, the road to hell is paved with pictures which are
not sincerely felt.

[On Convictions] Having made up your mind about the subject and
the style, *follow your convictions*. If you really feel a preference for
Corot's landscapes, for example, don't let anyone tell you it is out of
date, and if you *follow your convictions* without deviation, the world
eventually will beat a path to your doorstep . . . . Therefore, have
the *courage of your convictions* and *paint what and how you like*.

What marvelous insight—to perceive within each artist a
talent which finds its ultimate and most sublime expression
when it is true to what it is.

Although we may readily affirm the truth revealed here
about those who lead, are creative, or burn with the crusader's
heart, the idea that this principle could apply to Norman Average may strike you as somewhat of a stretch. Untrue!

When you see any person really well suited for his job, you
will find the kind of harmony between that person's Motivational Pattern and the job or role or expressions or form which
is being pursued by the person. A mother with the right kind
of moves—simultaneously enchanting her husband, distribut-
ing tough love to the children, overseeing a taut but adequate
food budget, surrounding the family with beautiful colors and
arrangements and lighting and efficiency—is worthy of praise
indeed. She is true to her gifts and has found a marvelous
means for their particular and strenuous exercise.

What is true of *some* mothers is true of *some* sales representatives, restauranteurs, auto mechanics, musicians, teachers,

and quality-control analysts. When careers and jobs are well suited for their gifts, they are finely honed expressions of their design. If we will be true to our design, we will move into the right careers. We will find the exact mode or niche or vehicle or mechanism or means to express the unique thing within us.

19—A Work-Controlling Pattern

In the last chapter, we revealed that your Motivational Pattern would seek to lead you not only in a career direction, but also into the exact job or type of artisan, housewife, or worker which you will find of greatest satisfaction. Here we consider the principle that, given any job or role, the pattern literally controls how you perceive that job or role and at least try to perform it.

If a job can be performed by a person in accordance with his Motivational Pattern, he will strive to do so. Regardless of what the job actually needs, or others think the job needs, a person motivated to innovate will try to innovate. One motivated to organize will change the organization; one motivated to overcome will find a dragon somewhere; one motivated to build relations will concentrate on making friends; one motivated to perfect will start looking for rough edges. People will put all their best efforts into and attempt to perform, shape, and emphasize that part of the job which allows them to do what they are motivated to do. Why do you think one wife emphasizes a dust-clean environment—and the next one wades through two-days' dirty dishes to get a cup of coffee for a neighbor who today needs a friend?

You Will Try to Use Your Whole Pattern

The impelling force we are describing refers to the whole pattern—not only the "one motivational thrust," but the *relationships*, the *subject matter and circumstances*, and the *abilities*. For example:

The Closely Controlling Manager/Mother/Teacher. The manager/mother motivated to closely control his or her subordinates or children will find some way of doing so. Perhaps you can suggest school for a week (or a year). You can lecture on modern management or motherhood to get agreement that he will delegate responsibility or she will take her hands off. Right? *Wrong!*

Somehow—someway—through some pretext of better communications, performance review sessions, or problems-of-the-week confabs, such an individual will end up with the hands back on. If direct attempts fail, there are many more subtle and not-so-subtle ways of getting and maintaining control. The same thing is true for the secretary's handling of her boss or the teacher's managing of her students. Somehow they will control the details of the other person's life.

The Individualist. The person motivated to operate as an individualist will find some way of functioning as *one*, in spite of his job responsibilities. You can make individualists— engineer, wife, minister, or linebacker—part of a team and they will seek a defined role which can be performed without being harnessed to others and where the results of their efforts are clearly traceable to the source.

A similar result occurs when the person motivated to operate as an individualist is made a manager of others. Many are, for frequently their excellence—preeminence at technology, the brilliance of personal performance, an ability to articulate what they know and think, an even moderate affability— makes them a prime candidate for promotion into the management ranks.

The individualist who is made a manager over others will find some way of performing as an individualist. This ranges from trying to do all the important work himself, to using others as his extensions, or to abdicating any continuing management responsibility and finding some project or problem which he can personally attack and perform—as an individualist.

The Team Member. Here is the team member who is placed in a position where he is required to operate alone. What the team member does is to look for someone in the neighborhood or the customer's organization with whom he can team up to do whatever else his pattern requires. That may work well or it may not.

There are a number of ways to invite trouble with the team member. He can be promoted into a key management position or he can be required to make a decision without some team around to consult and work with. In marriage, divorce—which is a serious enough rupture in itself—would be even more traumatic for the team member.

More Examples. Although creativeness frequently competes with motherhood as a desirable virtue, the person who is motivated to create or innovate will somehow perform his job in a creative way—regardless. This often includes breaking new ground where none is needed, making modest improvements at inordinate cost, and selling a modification of a project that does not generate profit.

A person motivated to learn by trial and error can dive into new products or new dishes without consulting the manual or the cookbooks. However, one motivated to plan in detail will have to be shoved off the cliff if action is required before he is ready.

If motivated to produce a product or some other visible evidence of one's effort, a man or woman will move towards those projects, redecoration problems, memoranda, policies, research, and development which have a large potential for completion and visibility.

If a staff member is motivated to be up with the big hitters, he will make recommendations which, if successful, will make him a big hitter—even when the suggestions are questionable in professional soundness. Finally, a wife will move to those parts of her role which represent a mess, confusion, and trouble—if she is motivated to bring order out of chaos.

Using Your Pattern—If You Have Room to Move

When any of us have room in which to move, we will move toward those things which allow us to exercise and fulfill our Motivational Pattern. When you get the opportunity, take a close look at how people in the same position perceive and perform in that position. Start with the teacher, housewife, waiter, clerk, service person. You will find the job being performed in vastly different ways, even though the position is the same.

Why does one person spend so much time and effort on *things*, another on *people*, and another on *economics?* Why does one concentrate on the planning-and-analysis parts of the job? Why does another spend most of the time on doing the job and none on planning? Why does that person emphasize relations with the neighbors or the front office and spend so much time away from his place of work?

People will perform their work in accordance with their Motivational Patterns—not what is needed or what is wanted (unless that is in the pattern)—but what they bring to it. If you are well suited for your role or job, application of your pattern assures delight to those you serve and satisfaction to you. To the extent that you are not well suited, you will give and receive more pain than pleasure.

20—A Life-Pervading Pattern

If you can get into the fine detail of your life, you will be amazed at the way it mirrors your Motivational Pattern. Your irritations, frustrations, anxieties, anger, depressions, and other troublesome emotions are triggered by the interaction of your pattern with the circumstances of your life—when you are crossed or blocked or otherwise unable to use your pattern.

- If you are motivated to get results, side issues can be an irritation—people who get in the way for too long can send you into a smoldering rage.
- If you are motivated to build relationships, people who move without considering others disturb you.
- If you are motivated to work alone, people who insist on teaming up with you will irritate.
- If you are motivated to plan carefully, a circumstance requiring you to wing it, can create much anxiety.
- If you are motivated to control everything that moves, late guests can ruin your evening.
- If you are motivated to keep everybody happy, confrontation can make you very uneasy.
- If you are motivated to convince others, friendly interruptions can turn you into an animal.
- If you are motivated to work with your own ideas, having to follow someone else's innovation can cool your cooperation.
- If you are motivated to counterpunch, having to take the lead can depress you.
- If you are motivated to work with tangible things, having to do a cost study can be a drag.
- If you are motivated to work with concepts, being asked to fix the furnace can depress you, later anger you, and then depress you again.
- If you are motivated to haggle, fair-trade prices can aggravate.

How you function within groups; how you react to what you hear and see; to what subjects you are drawn; what you actively reject; and what you are unconcerned about are determined by your Motivational Pattern. For example, your pattern shapes:

- What you get excited about when you read the newspaper.
- Your playing the devil's advocate; your always being on the inside; your always being on the outside looking in.

- Your tendency to wait until everybody else has had his say; your shooting from the hip; your defense of the underdog; your assault on the liberals.
- Your excitement about puzzles; your being drawn to Monopoly; your finding bridge dull (or exciting).
- Your entering of contests; your answering of ads; your willingness (or refusal) to follow standard instructions.

Your Motivational Pattern controls how you react to every situation with which you are confronted. Whether you respond, how you respond, the position you take, the role you seek, are all reflections of your pattern. Consider these examples:

- If you are confronted by a challenge, the pattern shapes whether you fight back, retreat to think it over, start seeking a compromise, or quickly build your defense.

- If you are confronted by a need, it determines whether you dig in your pocket, leap into the water, go back to reading your newspaper, start giving advice, or walk in the opposite direction.

- If you have to make a decision, your pattern controls whether you gather necessary facts, make a decision without deliberation, start looking for help, or identify several reasons why you cannot decide.

- If your child needs firm discipline, it shapes whether you start reasoning, crack some knuckles and then talk, seek some way of avoiding the problem, or accept any reasonable excuse.

Our causes—the issues we feel strongly about, for or against, and the things which tap our passions—are reflective of our Motivational Patterns. Realizing the self-serving quality of our nature (along with the blessing we can be to others) is the first step to mature manhood and womanhood. Hiding behind the rhetoric of righteousness or the goodness of our causes leads to personal or public war.

Knowing your pattern in detail will give you a practical understanding of why you function as you do. Anything you do which is based on something important to you is tied into your Motivational Pattern.

If you would like a more in-depth insight into how your Motivational Pattern pervades your life, answer the following questions. After you have, examine your answer in the light of your pattern, and see how clearly you now understand your conduct. Your sadness, elation, antagonism, anxiety, and feelings for—or against—reflect your pattern and your world— colliding or kissing.

1. Describe a situation in which you felt very frustrated. Include what you were trying to do, what happened, and how you felt.

2. Do the same thing with different situations where you felt anxious, elated, mad, or depressed.

3. If you want to go even further into the dynamics of why you move and feel as you do, note the obvious connection between your pattern and—

- How you handle money
- What you do with your spare time
- How you drive a car
- How you function in a group
- What you fantasize about
- How you handle the maintenance of your house, your car, your other possessions
- The organizations you join
- Whether you feel strongly about politics
- Your stand (if well developed) on abortion, equal rights, welfare, price supports, pornography—or any other issue

Part VI
Getting Down to Basics

When you have discovered your Motivational Pattern, you have simultaneously perceived that man does not act haphazardly. His behavior proceeds from an interior pattern which is intrinsic to his own nature. Realizing this, you now can probably appreciate much more fully our repetitive use of the word *design.*

Once we agree that the evidence shows man beginning with a design from early childhood and conclude that life will be fulfilling to the degree that an individual works in harmony with his design, we have several major questions to deal with.

1. If I am designed, who designed me?
2. What about negative factors such as psychological or emotional difficulties, laziness, or other personality flaws that may distort my design?
3. What are the implications for family life and society which impact so strongly on my behavior?

21—Who Designed Me?

An objective observer could conclude, after reading contemporary literature on the subject, that man is either an animal, or that man is a god who can shape and reshape himself at will, or somewhere between these extremes—that man can be conditioned into functioning as a responding automaton.

Are People Animals?

Mechanistic science proceeds under the assumption that people are animals, devoid of genuine willpower and—like rocks, galaxies, frogs, and apes—are governed by principles which can be discovered through properly conceived and executed experimentation. This approach to human behavior has failed to achieve any significant body of knowledge useful in understanding the behavior of the individual.

It has failed because it has not discovered any principle which governs all people and each person. It rejects and will, in po..it of fact, not even look at facts which conflict with its assumption. It represents what to us looks like a rather narrow adherence to a man-as-an-evolving-animal-so-there-must-be-some-uniform-principles theory which has controlled scientific research into human behavior.

Are People Gods?

At the other end of the spectrum, are the humanists who advocate a theory that a person can be what he himself decides, that he can change his motivation, develop into a different person, change his spots if he prefers stripes.

Are People Automatons?

Somewhere in between the two extremes of mechanistic-science assumptions and the gossamer world of the humanist is the world of behaviorism. A major branch of that world rests on the concept that a person's behavior is not caused by any unique personal quality which is resident within him, but is caused by the consequences of his behavior.

The theory can be spun so intricately—with such exquisite hypothecation, so glib, so believable, so inviting. But when we look for the supporting evidence—when we examine our own lives and conduct and that of those we live with and work with—we realize that it is not true. It is simply not possible!

There is no evidence, in the hundreds of cases with which we have worked, that anything or anybody or any circumstance can condition or otherwise cause a change in the Motivational Pattern. In the hundreds and hundreds of people with whom we have worked over an eighteen-year period, WE HAVE YET TO DISCOVER A SINGLE PERSON WHO DOES NOT DEMONSTRATE UNCHANGING CONSISTENCY IN HIS OR HER BASIC BEHAVIOR PATTERN.

The only way a person can be "motivated" or "conditioned" or "manipulated" is to get a hook into the preexistent Motivational Pattern and provide a "conditional" technique that exploits it. In spite of the hundreds of conditioning-reinforcing contingencies a person meets in life, he or she consistently selects only certain ones which are found to be of motivating value—and ignores all others, in spite of their intrinsic worth or popular appeal. Those certain ones are to be found in the person's Motivational Pattern. Any evidence proposed to the contrary is certain to exclude the demonstration of normal people engaged in normal activities or real-life circumstances.

The Failure of Theories

Although the above three schools of thought are deeply imbedded in our society and have consumed enormous amounts of energy, skill, and money in theoretical pursuits and experimentation, they have not been especially fruitful as far as everyday living of common people is concerned.

An obvious area of failure is in the area of career directions, where, of all places, most help is needed. It is not as if nothing has been invested in career research. The widespread need has required and received much attention on the part of private and federal agencies, but as those we have contacted who are knowledgeable about career research and education have admitted, the research is extensive and the practical results minimal.

A Divine Design

The assumptions made by those involved in the various theoretical schools concerned with human behavior are, for the most part, secular in nature. We believe room should be made for the consideration of a divine design.

If the basic design of man is not determined by environmental forces, but is imbedded in his own nature, a logical conclusion is that heredity is the source. This, in turn, can be viewed as another development in the vast evolutionary drama of man. Consideration of heredity as the source is certainly an acceptable idea to us; the evolutionary factor is not. Our reaction is based on a fairly homely idea which we will nevertheless admit.

We do not believe the larger can be totally derived from the smaller, the complex from the primitive. It would require an extraordinary leap of faith for us to embrace the idea that the intricate beauty of man's design has its ultimate origin in the primordial mud of the evolutionists' theory, a leap we are incapable of making.

We look for a prototype and believe we find it in the economy of God.

> Thou it was who didst fashion my inward parts;
> thou didst knit me together in my mother's womb.
> I will praise thee, for thou dost fill me with awe;
> wonderful thou art, and wonderful thy works.
> Thou knowest me through and through:
>   my body is no mystery to thee,
> how I was secretly kneaded into shape
>   and patterned in the depths of the earth.
> Thou didst see my limbs unformed in the womb,
>   and in thy book they are all recorded;
>   day by day they were fashioned,
>   not one of them was late in growing.
> How deep I find thy thoughts, O God,
>   how inexhaustible their themes!
>   *Psalms 139:13–17* NEB

It is true that a person can be distorted by parents or society, and true that inauspicious experiences of the past encrust us and blunt our joy, but even our reason is compelled by the suggestions of this Psalm to see that there is an inexplicable wonder about us that implicates God as our Designer.

22—*Ultimate Loving*

If God is the Prime Designer, then whoever He is cannot be less than what He designed. When we contemplate the genius involved in the creation of the human mind and personality, it is reasonable for us to assume that God is in some ultimate way a personal God and can be expected to communicate with His creations.

History shows that God has not only spoken, but has involved Himself in man's history. The drama of the Jews' contending with God in the monumental battle of wills portrayed in the Old Testament, is more than poetry or legend. There is a peculiar passion about those stories which convinces us that Abraham and Moses were not conversing with an illusion.

The battle of wills extends into the New Testament with the stunning command of Jesus Christ that we love others more than ourselves, that we wish others' good more than our own. It seems an impossible requirement, but one that is powerfully justified, especially in view of the compulsive nature of each person's Motivational Pattern.

The issue does not rest in a comparison of "good" Motivational Patterns versus "bad" ones. The problem is that *all* patterns are compulsively self-centered. Even patterns which cause individuals to serve and help, though they appear to be virtues, are in actuality additional demonstrations that people have a compulsive drive to satisfy their own motivations.

When theologians speak of man as a fallen race, they mean that the desires of every person who comes into the world are turned toward *self,* with no internal power available to reverse that self-gaze. Selfishness, war, and corruption are but symptoms of a spiritual disorder which thousands of years of progress have failed to eliminate, and these failings have continued to appear in our individual daily living.

We seek to be worshiped and exalted, to be above others. We strive to do the impossible. We wish to be envied, responded to, talked about, noticed, and treated as special. We want others to conform to our will; whereas we want to do what we want to do—when we want to do it.

We try to twist everything we voluntarily do in life into something which will serve our purposes. We even try to ignore our sublime design, so that we can call ourselves gods who are self-created. We ignore our derivative nature.

Karl Menninger, the eminent psychiatrist, has written a book entitled *Whatever Became of Sin?* in which he catalogues much individual and collective sin with a brand of intellectual honesty, wonderfully fresh and penetrating. He identifies the basic nature of man for what it is—self-centered—selfish—egocentric.

The human race has been beguiled into the fantasy which would make man God. All of us find such a prospect too tempting to turn away from. People in all walks of life, blinded by the power of their gifts—as if those gifts were self-created—have been led down a road which leads nowhere. What, under God, can be fruitful, joyous, creative, and sacrificial has become, under man, eventually empty, dull, and ultimately worthless.

The deadly lie hidden in all this is the assumption that people have the resources within themselves to become what they decide to become. Can a man or a woman make it by relying upon the resources within them? Many try. We all lust after what satisfies us and become anxious and frustrated when we cannot have it, are bored when there is no opportunity for attaining it, and wary about whether we can sustain it when we do have it. Then, in reaction, we may attempt to deny our motivations and either try to control all the variables in life or strive on and learn to live with anxious toil while others ignore responsibility and live to indulge themselves.

We repeat: Can mankind make it by relying on the resources within him? There is a mountain of evidence which mocks the attempt. A Motivational Pattern is a divine gift. Because of *our* nature it is also a curse. We cannot, by ourselves, eliminate that curse. Even the more brilliant, imaginative, stable, hardworking, and compassionate of mankind's representatives can do no more than extol the paradise that might be . . . *if.*

Who will help us become what we were created to be and deliver us from our failure? Shall meditation, therapy, sensitivity training, assertiveness training, transactional analysis, mind dynamics, group sex, a Ph.D., drugs, discipline, dialogue, or positive thinking free you to be what you are? If you think so, read no further. You have found your "messiah."

As for us, we are not going to add a new salvation to the above list. We are going to point to the image that has haunted the mind of man since history first reverberated with the astounding death of *one* man who claimed to be the Son of God and went on to deny the permanence of death. Yes, probably like you, we have been educated. We too are fluent in the sophistications of our culture and so are aware of all the deadly institutional distortions and stupidities that have been enacted ostensibly in the name of that One—but civilization in even its most brilliant stages has not delivered to us anything as compelling as the transforming power to which Christ directs us.

We have seen God work in lives and have watched compulsive self-love converted to freedom. It has happened often enough and radically enough to convince us of its reality. God has engaged the problem of man's egocentricity and has done so in a most profound way. He has initiated a radical possibility called *redemption.*

Granted, it is often used merely as a religious word, but its actual meaning is splendidly hopeful and full of love.

Redeem *means "to regain possession."* People are made to love ultimately. Our songs, poetry, legends—even those of popular culture—express the desire for an ultimate object for our love. The only One who by nature deserves such love is God. When we are willing to be set free from compulsive self-love, He gives us the power to turn our eyes from ourselves and fasten them on a far more wonderful object— Himself. That, in turn, creates in us a freedom to love others and ourselves—freely! We allow ourselves to belong to God and, in that relationship, to discover the possibility of acting according to "oughts" instead of "wants." As we mature in this relationship, we become increasingly free to do what we ought. The motivated design can then be exercised as a genuine gift, no matter what the pattern is.

Redeem *means "payment of amount due."* All of us agree that justice should always triumph; people ought to pay for their wrongs. Such justice should include the wrongs of our own self-centeredness. The whole message of the Old Testament is that they *can be paid for*—and that of the New Testament is that they *have been paid for.* Investigation of that mystery can deliver us from crippling guilt, remembering that the question here is not whether or not we like this idea or whether or not it is popular. The only question to consider is whether or not it is true.

Redeem *means "to rescue or deliver from bondage."* Jesus Christ once said that if you are willing to give your life away, you will save it—and if you hold on to your life, you will lose it. This paradox is applicable to our understanding of Motivational Patterns. When we are willing to give our basic abilities to God, to let Him do with them as He wills, we can trust that He knows what will make them fruitful in an ultimate way. He can deliver us from the bondage of our selfishness or the illusions of altruism and create in us a new experience—that of becoming what we were originally created to be.

There is a crucifixion we must share in, for real life to appear. This principle not only applies to the gifts we are able to use, but also has application when circumstances prevent their exercise. It can release us from resentment which could otherwise accumulate when things do not go our way.

Redeem *means "to fulfill."* Since God is the Designer of our basic Motivational Pattern, we can expect Him to work in harmony with His own intention in us and bring us into fulfillment on His terms, the terms that make final sense. The Apostle Paul once asked us to consider what it might mean "If God be for us . . ." (*see* Romans 8:31). What if it is true that God not only intends to set us free from the bondage of self-will, but that He also intends, with a passion that is stronger than ours, that we be fulfilled because He loves us?

The above ideas may be a problem for anyone who has a secular view of life. We can appreciate the difficulty it might pose, but as we face the evidence about human nature and the claims of Jesus Christ, we are forced to take seriously the provision available to us in dealing with its perplexities. All of our studies lead us to the conclusion that it is pointless to make the effort to study man, to understand him, and to improve his behavior without reference to his spiritual dimension. It is a violation of the fundamental scientific principle of examining all the available evidence, as senseless as ignoring the wind when we study the weather.

23—The Negatives

People sometimes become confused when we state emphatically that Motivational Patterns cannot change. They have seen others become more skillful by practice. They have seen people discipline their emotional lives and become happier. They have seen underdogs win and become successful and have seen stockbrokers move out of the city and become farmers. Surely each of these is a change.

It may be useful once again to compare the nature of your motivational design to the given nature of your physical design. What you are physically is quite arbitrary. What you do with it is not. But whatever you do with it, you cannot change the original stuff of who you are. If you are born white, you never will be black. If you are born short, you never will be tall. If you are born blue-eyed, you never will be brown-eyed. You can, however, change sloppy posture, exercise to keep yourself trim and more effective, and get rid of excess weight. In short, the ninety-two-pound weakling can change—not by becoming a different person, but by becoming more of what he ought to be.

Laced throughout the lives of people who are well suited, moderately suited, or poorly suited for their jobs is a whole series of additional encumbrances which stand between the person and an abundant life. The catalog is large! Many have bad work methods, compulsive personal habits, abrasive mannerisms, emotional problems, physical ailments or fear of them, strife on the home front, excesses, neurotic behavior, areas of immaturity, the lies of yesteryear, inadequate background, areas of little discipline, fears, and anger.

In spite of the vast evidence, no one should attempt to justify the negatives of his or her life with the idea of "That's how I am put together, and that is how you have to take me. It's part of my pattern, and that's not going to change."

There are improvements in the pattern required by its application in real-life pursuits and circumstances. Some examples follow:

1. The tennis player, desiring to excel, who has the big serve, the crackling forehand, and the brilliant net game—all of which are almost raw motivated ability—must stop running around his backhand and work hard at developing a competent stroke, if he wants to move beyond his local tennis club.

2. The youth who, at the age of twelve, astounded everybody by constructing a commercial-quality TV set without a kit, will end up as only a good technician, unless he submits his pattern to the discipline of a professional education.

3. The singer with the big, beautiful, high notes—and the motivation to make the Met—does not stand a chance to get even close unless she submits her gifts to the discipline of years of practice and learning how to sing softly and flexibly and in the lower range, too.

A Motivational Pattern is not static in the variety of its application. Nothing in the universe is. To be human beings means that we are in a process of time that provides opportunities for us to become more of who we are supposed to be. Knowing how we are designed provides us with wisdom as we develop a strategy for our lives. The world is not going to suddenly recognize our design and somehow accommodate us and eliminate the pain and the risk of being a human being—but there can be a big difference as to how we engage the world.

Laziness, hostility, insecurity, hatred, suspicion, anxiety, frustration, and obsessions are found in every person and they can cripple. Such qualities are part of everyday life and make it difficult or, in the extreme, impossible for a person to make productive use of his strengths. They are deformities of the pattern. One person knows he can sell but is afraid to risk rejection. Another individual never submitted his gifts to the discipline of education and is anxious that his ambition will be thereby disappointed. He finds himself attempting to bluff his way through, talking louder, pretending to understand, and hoping nobody catches on.

We have already discussed egocentricity as the root cause

for the basic crippling of man and have suggested how it can be dealt with. Beyond that is a need for a maturing process which requires discipline and often the help of others to encourage us, help us, or, in severe cases, to provide us with professional therapy.

Part VII
Benefits and Applications

24—To Name a Few . . .

How have people benefited from knowing their characteristic Motivational Pattern?

The immediate benefit realized by most people is a conviction that they are worthwhile, that they really have something specific to offer life.

A related second benefit has been a clarification as to whether or not one's life is headed in the right direction. If not, an individual has a reliable measuring stick to use in redirecting himself.

Third, an immediate advantage can be an explanation of the past: why certain jobs and roles and relationships and situations have been great, some okay, and some bad; why there has been failure, success, or near misses.

The fourth benefit has been an individual's insight into the details of why he functions as he does. Here the person can see his whole system of behavior: how he perceives his work; how he approaches it; what he emphasizes; what he rejects; whom he moves toward and why; whom he does not have time for and why; why he drags his feet on what issues; why he is responsive to certain assignments and avoids others; what kinds of problems he leaves unsolved and what he attacks.

An additional benefit has been a penetrating understanding of the usually hidden details of the inner emotional life. For example: Why does he get angry at other drivers? Why can't he stand being told how to do something?

Still another benefit has been the helpful insight which patterns can shed on the domestic scene. Each area of conflict, felt weakness, voids in relationships between husband and wife—and parent and child—is opened to solution by the understanding of the causative dynamics which are manifested in Motivational Patterns.

Other benefits can be those which shed light on such central matters as the person's faith in God, understanding of the nature of God, the kind of denomination and church to which one is drawn, the role played in the church, and the theology to which he is drawn.

Specific Applications

What have people done with all this insight? Even a fairly superficial understanding clarifies much we otherwise could not understand. A thorough, detailed understanding can be used to great advantage. A few of the specific ways Motivational Patterns are used:

HIGH SCHOOLS AND COLLEGES

- Help teenagers make decisions about college, vocational school, or work
- Reveal to teachers what and how (and if) each student will learn
- Give schools a clear selection method of determining who is motivated to teach and who is not
- Give college students a way to understand and draw out what their teacher has to say on a subject the serious student needs to learn
- Help college students identify the kinds of work, bosses, organizations, conditions, and goals they would find of motivating value

FAMILY LIFE

- Help singles consider some of the practicalities of getting married to one another
- Help married couples build their relationship on the reality of their patterns, and thus avoid possible conflict in household decisions
- Help young women decide whether or not they would be satisfied having and caring for babies
- Give parents a practical means to understand and guide their children

WORLD OF WORK

- Help managers improve their ability to select employees suitable for the jobs open and build organizations on complementary strengths
- Give an employee a practical means for increasing his work satisfaction, for evaluating what's wrong and what's right about his current job
- Help an organization find the source of poor performance by an individual or a group

THOSE LOOKING IN

- Give underemployed minorities, non-college graduates, and females a sound and saleable basis to define, locate, and land the right kind of job
- Give people out of society a solid, contributing basis for taking their place in our midst

The great variety seen in the application aspects of Motivation Patterning is not due to an attempt to include the universe in this one perspective. The diversity of application of Motivational Patterns is simply due to its extreme foundational nature. It is unavoidably basic. As an illustration, consider how central these patterns are in the matter of careers, relationships, and culture, as outlined in the next three chapters.

25—*Your Place in the Work World*

When you understand your Motivational Pattern, you understand what you should do with your life, that is, find work or activity which allows you to use your Motivational Pattern. Since there are literally thousands of job categories in our country alone, it is difficult to make a translation from a pattern to all likely careers and jobs.

However, there are a number of career and job implications contained in a Motivational Pattern which we want to note for you, and which should be used as a guide in your career planning and job decision making. Regardless of where you are in your career, you can benefit from considering or reconsidering the following points.

You will need at least one and perhaps several source books about employers in the geographic areas of interest to you. Ideally, your source material will show the products or services supplied, the kinds of jobs or work involved at some level of detail. If you combine the federal government's *Occupational Outlook Handbook* put out by the U.S. Department of Labor (which gives excellent detail on many occupations) with local or regional manufacturers' listings, you should have enough to work with, as a start. Besides its direct help, this handbook provides references to other sources of information. If you need more information and have run out of ideas, ask the reference librarian in the largest library near you.

Putting Your Pattern in Perspective

While the Motivational Pattern is essential to the career-planning process, it must be understood to be used properly. First, it is a picture of your requirements for satisfaction in work or leisure-time activities.

Second, it is an isolated picture of you. While some patterns immediately suggest a job to a keen observer, it is more commonly true that people are not neatly created to fit cookie-cutter jobs. It is helpful here to reread the chapters on pattern identification (Part IV) and review all the things you are not.

Third, your pattern can be well expressed in a number of different jobs. Therefore, you may end up staring at the pattern and saying, "Well? So what? Some implications are obvious, but how do I make a job decision with it?"

Fourth, the pattern becomes obviously useful as soon as you have something to measure it against: a job, a demand on you, the Motivational Pattern of a close friend, a course of study. Immediately you will be able to see why you are frustrated with a situation, a job, another person. You will be able to identify jobs that are right for you and others that do not fit the bill. See if you can identify the problems and potential in these situations.

- Person motivated to *build relationships* is offered a job as staff sergeant in charge of training in Marine boot camp . . . .
- Sally, who likes to work with *numbers or data,* is asked to write a promotional pamphlet for her division . . . .
- George, who is *individualistic* and independent of authority, is asked to be one of six on a subcommittee . . . .
- Fred, who likes to *build and develop,* gets in on the ground floor of a new company . . . .

You will be faced with dozens of decisions like these throughout your working life. Armed with your Motivational Pattern, you can make solid decisions that will yield personally fulfilling results. So let's start walking.

Step One: Establish a Job Objective

Knowing what you are looking for will help you find it. Many a person who wants a job, a different job, or something to do with his life doesn't know what he is looking for. So the first thing you do is establish what you have to give to an employer, which is the same thing, when understood properly, as what you want out of life.

However you want to look at it, the way you define your job objective is to synthesize the elements of your Motivational Pattern into a single statement. There are many ways of pulling those pieces together, but here is one approach you can use:

1. *A job working with* . . . . (Here insert your *subject matter:* people, ideas, numbers, structural things, and so on.)
2. *The conditions of the work* . . . . (Here insert your *circumstances:* are project oriented, require operating under stress, allow some freedom of movement, and so on.)
3. *Where I can operate* . . . . (Here insert your way of *operating with others:* as a member of a team, in a defined role, or in a leadership capacity.)
4. *Using my motivated abilities to* . . . . (Here insert your *abilities:* investigate for the facts, analyze their significance, improvise a solution, organize others involved, oversee the implementation.)
5. *Which leads to* . . . . (Here insert your one *motivational thrust:* a finished product, chance for advancement, greater responsibility, recognition for my contribution.)

In filling out this format, use whatever filler words make it flow and communicate your strengths in a clear, easily understood manner. In its "almost finished" form, it should look like one of the following:

Job Objective: A job working with people, merchandise, and money—where *the conditions of work* are not too structured and allow me to tackle and solve problems that come up, and require me to keep a cool head in the face of a lot of pressure; *where I can operate* pretty much on my own; *using my abilities* to evaluate people, make friends with them, sell them on myself and my product, keep my merchandise neat and orderly and carefully account for my sales and cost of sales; and *which leads to* opportunity for participation in the ownership or profits of the business.

Job Objective: A *job working with* machinery and its maintenance—where *the conditions of work* make clear what is expected of me, and each job can be completed before going to the next; *where I can operate* with others as part of a team; *using my abilities* to learn how new machinery works, set up a maintenance schedule, repair broken parts, improvising with what is available, and explain to operators how to properly use the machinery; and *which leads to* opportunity to work with greater variety and complexity of machinery.

What now is needed to complete your job objective (beyond synthesizing the pieces of your Motivational Pattern as in the examples above), is a reference to one or more specific industries or businesses or activities (and ideally, jobs or at least functions) within the named organizations. For example, in the first case: "A job in sales, customer service, or sales-training function for a retail business selling tangible products, working with people." Or, perhaps, as in the second case: "A job in maintenance or industrial engineering in the machine-tool or equipment-manufacturing industry, working with machinery."

In order to get this specific, you need to screen potential employers in the geographical area you live in or have selected. The next step shows several ways to do that.

Step Two: Identify Potential Employers

Start With Subject Matter. First, look at the subject matter with which you are motivated to work. That will usually help you make some general cuts. Take one element of the subject matter with which you are motivated to work and identify every industry, business, or other organization or profession where that subject matter is of central concern. For example, if *hardware or equipment* is your first screening element, you would include some and eliminate most of the possibilities, simply on the straightforward basis of what they are or are not. A foundry; a car dealer; different manufacturers of screws, electronic instruments, or pneumatic devices; manufacturers' representatives of plumbing supplies, pumps, or farm implements; construction and maintenance department of a municipal government; dealers in air conditioning, heating equipment, or office machines; a trucking firm; appliance-servicing business or machine tool shop would be examples of the first cut you could make of possibilities in your area.

Next, take a second element of the subject matter with which you are motivated to work and go through the possible employers which survived your first cut. If your second element is *enterprise or business,* for example, you would tend to eliminate any government departments or large organizations with no opportunity for an entrepreneurial spirit to thrive. Later, as you look more closely, you will probably eliminate family-held businesses where relatives hold all the key positions (unless of course, you want a few years of experience) and other organizations with similar attitudes about newcomers.

Next the Circumstances. After you have gone through each element in your list of subject matter, then consider the circumstances or context within which you are motivated to work. For example, if *new or novel situations* are of motivating value to you, the list of organizations surviving previous screening would be included or excluded on the basis of whether or not the nature of the product involved some new or novel feature. For example, you might, on this basis, include automobile sales and service and exclude the trucking firm; include the manufacturer of electronic instruments and exclude the screw manufacturer; include appliance servicing and exclude the plumbing-supply house.

Proceeding in this fashion, you should be able to screen out many possibilities and include others. Once you have identified likely industries or other employers, you can now proceed to consider functions and types of jobs within those organizations.

Step Three: Identify Potential Jobs

Here you will look at the most critical feature of your Motivational Pattern which must be satisfied in your work for you to find it of value—your *motivational thrust* or "one result." Many jobs accommodate a variety of motivational thrusts. For example, the position of salesperson could accommodate a motivation to win or prevail, to gain response, or to serve and help. What is helpful, therefore, about this part of the screening process is not pinning down one job, but identifying a few jobs that could accommodate your thrust—and also many that could not.

Now take your central motivational thrust and consider each kind of job available with the potential employers identified in Step Two. If you don't have this information, consult the *Occupational Outlook Handbook* referred to previously. Locate the kind of industry or other organization which you have identified as a potential employer and read about the various occupations employed in that industry. The chart on the next 2 pages will give you some idea of how to relate jobs to your one motivational thrust. Examples are given for several central motivations, listing potentially "right" jobs and also those which would probably be "wrong."

Whatever your motivational thrust, there are functions and jobs which would more clearly promote its fulfillment than others. Most are quite obvious if you hold your motivational thrust against the jobs in question. Usually, it's either "quite likely" or "unlikely." The critical point is knowing your thrust and asking the question.

So far you have: (1) a job objective; (2) some potential employers in your area; and (3) some possible jobs to explore. Now you need to know in finer, more accurate detail what these jobs really require.

Step Four: Determining the Critical Requirements of a Job

Discard the notion that employers know what they're looking for when they hire someone. It is an unusual event when a boss can clearly lay out all of the critical requirements of a job.

Central Motivation	Right Work		Wrong Work	
Fulfill Expectations/ Meet Requirements	Mother Customer service Production worker	Buyer Auto mechanic	Research scientist Long-range planner	Anthropologist Creative artist
Win/Prevail	Salesperson Collective bargainer Politician	Contract admin. Oncologist Bill collector	Customer service Counselor	Nurse Architect
Serve/Help	Clergy Waitress Funeral director	Appliance repairer Recreation worker	Credit manager Claims investigator Investigative reporter	Auditor Quality-control representative
Pioneer/Explore	Research scientist Marketing professor Research worker	Artist Writer Chef	Stock clerk Traffic manager Nurse	Pharmacist Loan officer Route driver Elevator operator
Master/Perfect	Plasterer Jeweler Tool/die maker Pilot	Dentist Pharmacist Bookbinder	Desk clerk Mother Medical (GP) Short-order cook	Buyer Loan officer Retail salesperson

Shape/Influence	Psychologist Barber Teacher Bartender	Clergy Public-relations representative	Assembler Mail carrier Telephone operator	Bookkeeper Taxi driver
Gain Response/ Gratitude	Teacher Field service worker	Social worker Mother Entertainer	Umpire Quality assurance representative	Judge Salary admin. Biographer
Build/Develop	Mother Engineer Ceramicist	Farmer Teacher	Payroll clerk Housewife Truck driver	Plant maintenance worker
Acquire/Possess	Entrepreneur Forester	Recruiter Real-estate salesperson	Clergy Product planner Cashier	Patrol officer Politician Researcher
Gain Recognition/ Visibility	Model Waiter Receptionist Entrepreneur	Retail sales rep. Entertainer Trial lawyer	Cost accountant Housewife	Typist Farmer

It is certainly a common experience when a person takes a job, assumes that he will have certain duties, and then finds out that those duties take up a minor portion of his time. Titles are often smoke screens that hide actual critical requirements.

It is usually not true that employers are trying to hide the real requirements; they just are not accustomed to thinking about them. However, you can cause employers to think about and reveal critical requirements. There are actually two levels of analyzing these requirements:

1. Eyeballing It—This is actually no analysis at all, but it can be an effective way of making a rough cut in planning job decisions. If a job has relatively simple functions, this could be as far as you need to go. While performing your "armchair analysis," consider these points:

- What *abilities* are required?
- What will I be working with (*subject matter*)?
- What are the working *circumstances?*
- What will be my working *relationship* with others?
- What is the essential nature of the work?

2. The Critical-Requirements (CR) Interview—While it is true that you may not be able to perform it until you are being considered for a job, the CR interview ideally should be conducted with the employer's representative and the person currently in the job or who performed it or a similar job previously. The interview with the employer is very similar to a SIMA interview in that you try to get past superficialities and down to the essential requirements (details)!

EMPLOYER:	You'll be *supervising* a small office.
YOU:	What do you mean by *supervising?*
POSSIBLE ANSWERS:	(a) Making sure others in office keep working
	(b) Monitoring traffic flow on a chart
	(c) Supplying typists with paper clips and ribbons
	(d) Emptying the garbage, replacing light bulbs

This may seem ludicrous, but as we said previously, many job titles merely hide the real duties that are critical to your job.

The interview will have to be more indirect with the employer than with the former jobholder. You don't want to antagonize a prospective boss. In either or both cases, try to pin down the same details that you were after when simply eyeballing the situation:

Ask for examples or illustrations of each critical requirement. When the example is given, probe the details of how it is done, much the same way achievements are probed. For example:

- "What's involved in handling the customers?"
- "How do you go about setting up your day's run?"
- "What are the detailed steps in making such a survey?"
- "What do you mean by coordinate?"

Step 5: Matching You and the Job

After you have a handle on one or more jobs, you are in a position to compare what you have and want to give with what the job requires. Each part of your pattern and each ingredient of each part should be held up to the critical requirements of the job(s) being examined.

Relationships With Others as a Long-Term Consideration. A most critical input in this selection process is how you operate with others. For example, if you are an individualist, do not select or move to a career requiring you to "become" a manager for you to succeed. Instead, select a career which accommodates growth as an individual contributor and provides appropriate challenges and rewards throughout the length of your career. Look down the road which you are poised to select—and understand the jobs to which it leads. Are you right for those jobs? Find out about them. Also make your decisions on more than the first job. It will only last a few years, in all likelihood.

Less pronounced, but still critical, is what you plan and do if you are what we call a playing leader or a hands-on manager or a director. In all three cases, your climb up the managerial ladder is limited by how you operate with others and your need to be close to the action. So choose a career and particularly an organization which would tend to encourage its managers to stay on top of details. Do not get on an escalator onward and upward if you are not motivated to do so.

In your career thinking, try to anticipate this problem of being required to "become" something else to get ahead in your field. You will likely face the question sometime in your career and need to know how you will handle it and why your decision is right for you. You will need to defend yourself against all sorts of persuaders in your work and family life who would encourage you to be what you are not.

In addition to knowing whether or not you are likely to run with the pack, run alone, plan where the team should go, and so on, it is most important that you clearly understand and use in your career decision the following:

1. What kind of a person can you work for?
   ____ Any kind   ____ Hands-on   ____ Hands-off

2. If you are a manager of some sort, what kind of a person can best work for you?
   ____ Any kind   ____ Strongly dependent
   ____ Independent
   ____ Arms and hands   ____ Inexperienced

3. What kind of people do you work well with?
   ____ Any kind   ____ Same and higher levels
   ____ Mainly the "bright people"
   ____ Same and lower levels

Matching Your Abilities.   You need to understand your *motivated abilities* in keen detail to get as much out of your pattern as it can offer you in the career-planning process. If, for example, you love to learn new things, but learn mainly by doing, certain fields of work requiring a comprehension of underlying phenomena and principles would be a struggle for you. Check each ability in your pattern against the critical requirements of the jobs being considered.

Looking at Your Subject Matter Again. Ideally, you would search for and find a job with an organization where *subject matter* of motivating value to you was central rather than peripheral. For example: The insurance industry can make use of people who want to work with art and design, but it would hardly hold major long-term career opportunities for such a person.

Is the point clear? Try to move to a field of work and a specific organization and function where your subject matter coincides with foundational disciplines and functions. At least in the first five to ten years of your career, go where your subject matter is central, high priority, alive and growing. In these years, you need to lay the best groundwork you can assimilate. Almost every profession and trade and functional specialist benefits from a working apprenticeship under the tutelage of the experienced.

Similarly, Consider Circumstances. If *needs and causes* are in the "circumstances" part of your pattern, think carefully before going into a job not principally concerned with such matter. You can find yourself with negative, "anti" attitudes and cause yourself many problems. Get into a function and a job which tries to meet needs and causes with which you can identify.

If *projects* are in your pattern, try to get into a job and organization typified by projects and project-type or project-functional matrix organizations. Some types of businesses are inherently project-oriented: consulting firms, engineering-construction, research laboratories.

Do not take lightly the presence of *stress* circumstances or *combat or challenge.* Seek out work which inherently contains those kinds of circumstances, rather than work which provides them occasionally or can only be manipulated to do so. For example, many types of sales, development engineering, project management, labor relations, customer services, and commercialization typically present such circumstances.

Do Not Quit Yet. There are other items in your Motivational Pattern which can be helpful in your career planning. Typical of this kind of potpourri about you and your pattern would be things like having to work from your own ideas; having to prepare yourself thoroughly before you are tried; wanting to tie up all details on one job before you move on to the next; wanting help from your boss only at the beginning of a project; having to know clearly what is expected of you; needing a climate of acceptance within which to operate; controlling the detail of work performed by clerical or other supporting personnel. This kind of data about your pattern will enable wiser job decisions, fewer periods of anguish or boredom, and richer, fuller work and life.

Having Trouble Comparing Jobs and Patterns? In considering any job, ask yourself these questions:

1. What elements of my Motivational Pattern do I have to give that the job does not require or allow for?
2. What does the job or career require that I don't have?
3. Where is there a good fit?

Implications for Women Considering New Careers

A question frequently put to us is "Do women have Motivational Patterns suitable for careers outside of the home—or in management—or someplace other than where they are?" There is a concern that the "limited" nature of a woman's life up to the present has prevented her from becoming what she might otherwise have been.

Having read our findings about patterns, you will know the answer to that question. Regardless of the nature of her "job," each woman has found some opportunity to exercise her pattern somewhere in her life. Maybe her achievements have not been as full and abundant as they would have been in different work or environment, but she has most likely already been what she may want to be in some second career.

In other words, she has managed, created, controlled, persuaded, scheduled, organized, promoted, repaired, counseled, evaluated, negotiated, researched, built, planned, executed, interacted, presented, or performed—in one way or another, someplace in her life's activities, regardless of how well or how poorly her primary job fits her pattern. And she has found some way of acting independently of supervision, with others, by herself, as a coach, coordinator, director, manager, or whatever else is her motivated way of operating with others. Our advice to all—women and men—is that you should not move in a direction alien to what you have already been and achieved. Stay true to your gifts and motivations.

Help for All Ages

Consider the possibility of young men and women knowing their Motivational Patterns and the likely direction of their careers early in their lives. What a difference to the individual and society if education and work experience would aim at developing and accommodating Motivational Patterns.

What is so exciting about that potential for youth is also true, to some extent, for every person—regardless of age, sex, or color. Even the person in or approaching retirement, who has more history than future, can transform the twilight years from a waiting game to a productive and richly satisfying life.

So, if you are just getting started, are well along, midway, or on the downhill side of life, much is to be gained by you, those you live with, and those you serve—if you would take the time and effort to discover and make use of your Motivational Pattern.

26—*Discovering Relationships*

There is a tiresome truism frequently offered as a solution for clashing relationships, whether they take place on the job or at home. People repeatedly propose communication as the answer to discord. We observe, however, that people in conflict with others are often embroiled in an abundance of communication, much of it quite clear. But though genuine communication is obviously required to produce harmony between people, the emphasis is usually on the action, rather than the content, of communication. We believe what is being said is most important.

Christian principle insists that concern for the other party towers over any other feeling we may have in our relationships with others. Regardless of the truth for which we may be fighting or the importance of what justifies the conflict, there is no loophole for the extremity of Christ's teaching that we should love our enemies. So the most important message to communicate is that of caring, the kind that does not have a price tag attached.

Analyzing Relationships

Beyond this, we frequently discover the need for understanding some realities about people. Many times battles of principles camouflage a collision of Motivational Patterns. This realization alone should illuminate many of your relationships and provide the basis for practical strategy in moving in the most graceful ways possible with other people. But to develop further your grasp of how Motivational Patterns express themselves in typical job and family situations, we have devised a chart in which we propose a fictional Motivational Pattern for you and for people in your job and family. We would like you to play the role of detective and analyze the evidence in the chart on the next page, in order to describe

Person	One Result	Relation	Subject Matter Circumstances	Abilities
BOSS A	Master/ Perfect	Director	Numbers/Details Hardware Cost-Wise	Analyze Plan Proceduralize Control
BOSS B	Exploit/ Maximize	Manager	Technical/ Mechanical Constraints/ Deadlines	Investigate Organize Operate/Run Motivate/Inspire
SPOUSE	Gain Response	Team Member	People/ Relationships Art	Study Draw/Design Counsel/Advise Do/Execute
FATHER	Acquire/ Possess	Manager	Cost-Wise Details Physical/Structural Problems/Difficulty	Evaluate/Assess Strategize/Scheme Order/Organize Operate/Run
SON A	Make the Grade	Team Member	Group Activity Projects/Programs Presentations	Practice/Persevere Plan How Do/Execute Perform/Act
SON B	Serve/Help	Individualist Independent	Values/Ethics Needs/Causes People	Learn/Study Conceptualize Write Speak/Advocate
YOU	Innovate/ Pioneer	Individualist Independent	Concepts/Ideas Technical	Conceive Ideas Experiment Analyze Speak/Teach

the kind of relationship that would develop. (We are assuming that there are no neurotic factors to complicate the relationship.)

After you compare your fictional pattern with that in each relationship, attempt to sketch out what kind of problems, if any, would develop. Then look at our expectations and see how well you do.

Expectations

Boss A

You should never have gone to work for this person because he wants to manicure and you want to swing. You would like to work on the big picture and would hate the detail he expects.

The kinds of things you would argue about would include the budget he insists you work within, in spite of the fact you need more equipment to finish your project. While you are working three ideas down the line from the one your boss is concerned with, he wants you to set up some better methods so others can repeat your work. He also wants you to do things the way *he* wants you to do them and you want him to direct that which he knows something about.

We see no way of salvaging this relationship. You both could make warm, friendly attempts again and again to do so, but the individual patterns would again naturally clash. You should simply change jobs because neither pattern is going to change.

Boss B

If you were wise enough to change jobs and asked the right questions of Boss B during the job interview, you might have made a somewhat calculated guess that he would be a good person for you to work for. This boss would probably have a real interest in accommodating your way of working. There would be some uneasiness on his part about your keeping your agreed-upon objectives in mind and seriously trying to get them done. If your boss learns how you function—and there is more than a good chance he would—he will know when you reach critical points and encourage you to focus on a particularly likely solution.

The preceding are some of the more obvious observations. See what you might identify as likely areas of fit or misfit between YOU and your FATHER and each of your SONS. To aid your analysis, refer to the chart and attempt to answer the following questions:

FATHER

> How do you and your father get along?
> In what areas would he criticize you when you were a young person?
> What has his reaction been to your way of living?
> What has been his reaction to the way you manage your sons?
> Does he approve of your wife (husband)?

SON A

> What is your area of greatest criticism of your son?
> What do you do when he wants to spend time with you?
> What kind of activity have you found which you both draw close to?
> What might you do or suggest for him to do that would draw on his pattern?

SON B

> Why do you think you and this son get into so many heated discussions?
> Have you ever figured out why he is so anti-establishment?
> Have you ever figured out why he brings home so many sick cats, stray dogs, and people who are down and out?
> Why do you suppose he resists your advice about the direction for his life?

SPOUSE

You and your spouse would likely have a good relationship because she/he is motivated to get you to respond and to solve problems of a relational nature. She/he would probably take the initiative if you had to work out differences.

You can probably help come up with activities where you function together—which is so important to your wife/husband—but where you are free to operate in a more individualistic way. Consider, for example, where she/he scrapes off the wallpaper and you apply the new covering; where she/he takes care of the garden and you worry about the landscaping; or where you play an individualistic sport or hobby together (golf, ski, chess), where one has considerable competence in it and does not leave the other behind with her/his pioneering.

Now that you have some preliminary experience evaluating the impact of one fictional individual's Motivational Pattern upon that of another, you can take your real pattern and project some of the possibilities in your actual relationships. Use the diagram on the next page. In doing so, understand that the Motivational Pattern does not tell everything about a person. It describes the basic motivational design which is critically foundational, but a human being is a very complex organism. The Motivational Pattern does not intend to describe a person's emotional structure, though much of that may become apparent during a thorough interview. Motivation Patterning is not a psychological tool, and it would mean a serious distortion of its use to attempt to use it in such a way.

YOU

One Result

Fit/Misfit	Suggestions

One Result

Relation

Fit/Misfit	Suggestions

Relation

Subject Matter/Circumstances

Fit/Misfit	Suggestions

Subject Matter/Circumstances

Abilities

Fit/Misfit	Suggestions

Abilities

27—Implications for Society

Consider this one thought: any social, economic, or political institution dominated by one individual has imbedded in it not only the benefits of that person's abilities but also his distortions.

Government

No single person possesses the variety of Motivational Patterns required to run most institutions, whether they be corporations, churches, or countries. An individual may possess the leadership abilities vitally necessary for survival and growth, but if the institution totally revolves around the leader, there is sure to be evidence of distortion, in some cases to a crippling degree.

For this reason, the formation of boards of directors, committees, and other bodies to complement the function of the leader or authority figure is necessary to healthy functioning. The genius of the American political system is the recognition of the danger of centering on one individual. Political and legal checks and balances have been designed into governmental processes to protect against distortions in the use of power. The additional result is the possibility of complementary relationships not only between governmental agencies, but also between officials, with the strengths and weaknesses of one balancing the weaknesses and strengths of the other.

Business and Society

In the American economy, there is also the opportunity for the Motivational Patterns of individuals to be tested in ways which prevent permanent survival of distortions. The person who attempts to go into business without an entrepreneurial gift cannot survive if there is no artificial governmental support, as is the case in some countries. By nature, the free-enterprise system weeds out those who do not possess the specific gifts necessary for healthy business activity. Continued success requires a large number of gifts, including those of salesmen, managers, producers, organizers, craftsmen, designers—all of whom must come into a properly balanced organization in order to survive.

Man is social. It is impossible for him to become an individual by himself. It is a psychological necessity for him to discover himself in others, beginning with his family. The same principle extends itself to the social structures of human civilization. We need each other in order to function. We are dependent upon one another's gifts. No one person has them all. The more that structures within any society adapt themselves to the actualities of man's nature, the more effective they become for that society.

There are far-reaching benefits inherent in the practicalities of using Motivation Patterning in government, schools, and other agencies concerned with helping people. It provides a way to understand and bring about professional, governmental, and educational policies which enable individuals to use their gifts and so strengthen the society which gave them a rightful place. But there is also great danger in a society that fails in its concern for the individual.

Education

The largest benefit which mankind derives from education is its civilizing influence. In spite of the failures we might identify in our schools, there is, nevertheless, a transmission of civilizing assumptions from generation to generation which keeps us from rampant barbarism.

Because of this, it is reasonable to demand that all members of our society go through certain common educative experiences, especially those producing literacy. Compulsive education based on the traditional values of Western Civilization and combined with an understanding of the contemporary needs of society have survival implications deeply imbedded in them.

Regardless of the Motivational Patterns of our youth, it is necessary to require them to study that which they might not choose if they were given choices. It is necessary to expect large investments of their time to be given to learning activities which are not necessarily in keeping with individual designs. This necessity, however, must be reconciled with the fact that students tend to learn certain kinds of subject matter, to learn those subjects only in a certain way, and to learn in that way only to accomplish limited objectives.

There is no way a student who competes for grades is going to be transformed into a person who is motivationally a learner. If a student works for teacher approval, it makes sense to exploit that for optimum learning experiences for that particular student. No sermon about the value of learning for its own sake is going to change that child's need for teacher approval. The student who works for straight *A*'s may be doing so because it is a way to gain recognition, and if you eliminate grades, you may well be eliminating any further learning for him.

The way a student will learn has little to do with what the educational system determines. A student will learn precisely in that way he is designed to learn, and nothing anybody else decides will change him. Perhaps it is time to admit humbly that we ought to teach in ways that increasingly recognize the unique way each student is put together. It is the real teacher, by the way, who is more willing to yield to that truth.

A large number of those in teaching positions are not teachers by motivation. There are organizers, controllers, managers, actors, people who want to relate, and people who want to do a lot of things that have little to do with the learning process. We know by experience that teachers who have been identified as such, through Motivation Patterning, consistently teach and want real learning to take place and have no intention of doing anything else. This is true in private schools, Sunday schools, or public schools. Bring together a faculty whose Motivational Patterns give clear evidence that they are teachers, give them sound educational objectives, and you will have superb education going on.

What is most costly is the deadening effect which the educational process can have during and after school years. What should be a personally rich and rewarding experience is often lifeless and with little redeeming value. What should be a stretching, disciplining foundation to a lifetime occupation, is too often irrelevant to what could be a productive and satisfying career. A student can complete sixteen or more years of formal education and not have an understanding of his most central and dynamic qualities. The failure to recognize the unique design of each youth is disastrous. For by such failure to comprehend and equip the student for adult work and life during the years set aside for such purposes, the chances are more than even that the adult so ill equipped—and with such inadequate self-understanding—will spend his life running a race he is less than competent to run and really never meant to enter.

Implications for Parents

We know by experience that being parents is a risky yet wonderful process. We are involved with the shaping of values and character, as well as the development of hopes and the understanding of self-worth. We believe that all of these qualities will not only enhance our children's lives, but that they are factors in an eternal destiny. That one fact causes us to be serious in learning how to be effective as parents.

The dominant problems we have seen emerging out of a large number of counseling sessions with young people revolve around the principle we began with. Each person is already designed, yet many parents not only have a clear intention to make their children become what they as parents decide, but they see it as their duty to do so. What we are saying is that it is not only a futile exercise, but the attempt may seriously distort the direction of the child. It is not unusual to find parents giving or withholding love as a means to get the ends they desire. The clever parent does so in ways that not only prevent those outside the family from seeing this, but often diminish their own ability to see. Parents whose own

Motivational Patterns include either controlling, directing, or managing may be especially at fault here.

The corrective we would emphasize—in view of what we have learned in applying the knowledge gained from our work to the area of parent-child relationships—is pointed up in the parental choice to *control or confirm.*

It is safe to use the word *control* when we are dealing with obedience in a child, but in the context of his or her destiny, wise parents recognize the uniqueness of their child and learn how to *confirm* what has already been created. To do so, parental ambition for the child is replaced by an intention to discover evidence of what is positively fulfilling to the child, in even the small beginning experiences of play, and to patiently nurture the child's development.

There is a considerable degree of freedom in this approach since the false responsibility of determining the child's future is replaced by the exciting discovery of who God has created. In these terms, we are not responsible to our own hopes but to the requirement that God has a prior claim on our children and we had better recognize the way things are and give up our possessiveness.

As the child discovers who he is, he must learn to appreciate who he is. The evidence seems to point to parents as primary determiners of children's attitudes toward their own self-worth. Children will learn to appreciate their own gifts and motivations according to the way the parents teach them.

This confuses some parents who discover in their children a low level of self-esteem, in spite of all the positive affirmations given. What usually is occurring in such instances is that the child is responding in imitation of the parents' responses to their own gifts and motivations, rather than to the indoctrination of what is said. Dad may *say* that he does not impose a verbalized perfectionist standard upon his son. Meanwhile, he may be extremely demanding in his own work.

One of the healthiest attitudes parents can introduce into family life is that of gratitude. Parents should teach their children to be grateful to the God who designed them and to accept the gifts He has given. Parents can teach best, though, that which they have lived out themselves. When they have identified their own gifts, they can be specific about what they are grateful about and provide a potent way to teach children how to be joyful about themselves.

28—Final Words

Everything we are—and everything we have—comes from someone or something else. Our language, the food we eat, the structure of our thinking and our theology—all the stuff of our existence has other sources than ourselves. There is nothing original to us, and anything we create is in actuality the recombining of that which is already made.

Parental influence, socioeconomic environments, and heredity converge to program our future. Without God's intervention, we are required to act out this program of compulsive factors and produce what already is in us. He who is the Author of Creation has devised a means for us to become a "new creation." To be a new creation in Christ means that the old compulsive causal pattern is replaced by the power to become what God intended in creating us.

Amid mass communication and mass production and mass education, many people hunger to discover their own originality. They desire to be unique and attempt to pursue individuality. But, as George MacDonald once reminded us, our Lord never pursued originality. He was that by nature. We can only become unique when we become joined to the Body of Christ and therefore share in its nature.

God's raw material for man was mud. Similarly, the muck of our personal history, its disappointments, and its repeated self-seeking can become transformed by God. Let us trust Him to do that. There may be much evidence substantiating a spirit of hopelessness, contaminating our days with disappointment. It is useless to fight such feelings by pretending that the evidence is in error. Our fulfillment and joy do not rest in such evidence, but neither do they rest in spectacular positive accomplishments. We are to walk in faith, trusting God to take our gifts and abilities to produce in the end that which will be unique from His point of view. The results will be satisfying to God as well as to us, and incredible as it may seem, eternally so. *Those are stakes worth playing for.*

Appendixes

Appendix A—Questions People Ask

Don't people lie about their achievements?

No. They either are unable or unwilling to lie about achievements in a way which reveals a totally consistent, detailed picture of themselves throughout their lives. Our experience has been that people tend to understate rather than inflate their achievements.

Are Motivational Patterns really accurate?

Yes. The patterns are accurate. The achiever's spouse, friends, boss, and peers invariably agree on the essential accuracy of the pattern as true of the achiever in action. The level of detailed accuracy varies with the amount of detail given in describing the achievements. For example, assume we know a person is good at selling. To determine what kinds of products, what kinds of markets, what kinds of customers, what kinds of selling situations, how much and how frequently—we need a highly detailed account of his achievements.

By what standard is the achiever good at something?

"Better than most others" in the ability involved, and probably "outstanding" among his peers.

Isn't a person's image or self-understanding distorted?

Frequently. But the process does not call on or allow the person to relate his self-image. Instead, the person is asked to recall what he enjoyed doing and believes he did well. Once an enjoyable achievement is identified, the achiever functions almost as an objective reporter of what happened.

Does everyone have a Motivational Pattern?

Yes. We have found patterns for every person who has given us the basic achievement information. Only a few people have failed to give us the information needed, and these were people with serious emotional problems. We have worked with highly successful and very unsuccessful men and women, ages twelve to sixty-five; people with black, white, brown skin; people who have been raised in the United States and related cultures, some from Central America, others from the Middle East, and a few from the Far Eastern countries.

Do people enjoy the process?

Yes, but with qualification. Most all people find the experience most enjoyable once they have completed it. However, this is a totally new experience for 99 percent of those we have worked with. Many express embarrassment at having to deal with their good side.

Appendix B
SIMA—Biographical Information

name _____
address _____
_____
date _____

sima

System for Identifying Motivated Abilities

part one: biographical information

If you are like most people, you have never taken time to sort out the things you are good at and motivated to accomplish. As a result, it is unlikely that you use these talents as completely or effectively as you could.

Identification of your strengths and vocationally significant motivations is the purpose of SIMA.

To complete this form, you are asked to list and describe things you have done that you:
          1) **enjoyed doing**   and   2) **believed you did well.**
Such achievement experiences may have occurred in your work or your home life or your leisure time.

It is imperative that you put down what was important to **you**. Do not put down what you believe other people might think as important. Also, it is essential that you relate **specific** achievement experiences and not general ones. To help you understand the type of achievement experiences we are after, you will find on the next page examples of things other people have listed as personally significant.

There is no time limit to complete the form. IT IS NOT A TEST, so enjoy yourself. There are no right or wrong answers.

People Management Incorporated
Copyright 1963

summary examples

"Putting on plays for neighborhood children with costumes, props, etc. The most successful project was transforming a shed in back of our house into a fairyland with lighting effects, decorations, princesses, witches, etc."

"I built and mastered the tallest pair of stilts in my neighborhood. I started a stilt craze among my friends."

"I had a job as a printer's devil. I developed a method of cutting stereotypes which was faster and more accurate than that previously used."

"I established an evening routine of a quiet time of sharing and reading with our children which made bedtime an enjoyable end to the day."

"Was a prime mover in starting company. Saw utility of product concept. Had much to do with early market development. Helped conceive basic manufacturing concepts."

"Organized and ran a company-sponsored national conference with about 100 participants. Conference was a resounding success."

"While very young (4 — 6 years) I would work with my Dad in his workshop, helping him build things and clean up afterwards; with his help, I constructed several 'good' pieces of doll furniture."

"Raised over $10,000 in college fund raising campaign by telephone."

"Bought a relatively rundown house in a good neighborhood. Turned cost of about $10,000 into a value increase of about $6,000."

detailed examples of most important

"I guess I was 7 or 8 — I was always collecting animals — one day I walked into this crow — I guess it was a broken wing — I really wasn't sure — but it couldn't take off — so I carried it up stairs — had a bird cage — put the crow in there — so I took care of him — fed him and my dad helped me watch that the wing was all right — then after about a week or so, we just opened the little door and let the bird find his wings."

"The district I took over was never more than in one of the lowest 3 sales districts in comparative rank with others. Realization of quota was 15%. I began a detailed study of existing franchises and began anew. In 2 years my district was #1 and never dropped below 3rd place again."

"In course of constructing a working live steam model locomotive, built an extremely complicated reversing device following blueprints and using metal working tools and brazing equipment to complete part to very close tolerances."

"As field engineer on construction of prototype nuclear steam generator test facility, analyzed problem and reduced costs by nearly $2,000 by suggesting that ends of the piping be swaged down to a slip fit over the tubing nozzles and that a conventional socket weld then be made."

For each period, briefly describe two (or more) specific things you accomplished that you **enjoyed doing** and **believed you did well**.

Childhood
(a-1)

(a-2)

Teen Years
(b-1)

(b-2)

Age 18-22
(c-1)

(c-2)

Age 22-25
(d-1)

(d-2)

Age 26-30
(e-1)

(e-2)

Age 31-35
(f-1)

(f-2)

Age 36-40
(g-1)

(g-2)

Age 41-45
(h-1)

(h-2)

Age 46 and later
(i-1)

(i-2)

Of the things you have described, note in the boxes below (e.g. h-2, f-1) the six most important to you, not necessarily in order of importance

Taking the six most important achievements in the order given in the preceding boxes describe:

- HOW YOU GOT INVOLVED IN IT IN THE FIRST PLACE
- THE DETAIL OF WHAT YOU PERSONALLY DID
- WHAT WAS PARTICULARLY ENJOYABLE OR SATISFYING TO YOU

Start each paragraph by repeating the summary statement of the achievement

(   )

Appendix C
SIMA—Interviewing Procedures

```
name _____

address _____

       _____

date _____
```

sima

System for Identifying Motivated Abilities

part two: interviewing procedure

A SIMA Interview is important in order to get a more complete elaboration of a person's enjoyable achievement experiences. Many people talk better than they write. The interviewee should bring to the session a completed SIMA Part I — Biographical Information, which contains his written description of his enjoyable achievement experiences.

To conduct a SIMA Interview, you simply read what the interviewee has written and ask him to expand on it . . . Tell me the details of that achievement, how did you go about that? Tell me more about that. What was your part? Can you give more details about how you did that?

In a SIMA Interview you are after one thing . . . the details of how he did what he did . . . and what there was about what he did that he enjoyed. As the interviewee talks, you take notes and/or tape what is said.

WHAT TO AVOID

1. Avoid leading questions. Do not explore any area or walk through any door the interviewee has not opened. Do not ask any questions requiring an answer outside of the achievements the interviewer has listed.

2. Avoid leading questions. Do not explore areas of personal interest to you.

3. Avoid leading questions. Do not explore areas critical to the job for which he is being considered.

4. Don't conduct an interview by other rules. In a SIMA Interview, you do not have a two-way flow of communication; you do not try to win confidence through technique, manner or other artiface; you are not trying to give or get impressions; you do not play a role.

5. Avoid judging. All men do what they do to fulfill their own motivations. Some only appear to do otherwise.

SIMA PROCEDURE

FIRST — Simply explain the procedure you will follow: that you are after the details of how he di
what he described as achievements, and what he found enjoyable. Remind him the nature of SIM/
is to identify talent. If practical, give him an extra copy of his completed SIMA Part I for him t
follow as you proceed.

SECOND — Read the first achievement he described and say, "Tell me more about the details c
that." Keep milking the achievement until you have gotten all the details he can recall. Use suc
questions as:

> Would you give me more details of what you did?
> Give me an illustration of what you mean by "coordinating."
> Would you elaborate on one example of that?
> What was your role?
> Organize? What do you mean by that?
> What were you good at?
> How did you go about what you did?
> Tell me about that.
> Tell me more details of your part in that.
> What did you enjoy about that?

THIRD — Take notes as the interview progressess, moving from the earlier to later achievements:

- Pay careful attention to and note anything which describes the details of what he
  did, how he did it and what he enjoyed about it

- Especially note, verbatim if you can, words which reveal:
  > an ability used . . . "organized; sold"
  > a subject matter worked with . . . "machine; figures"
  > the nature of his relationship . . . "did all by myself"
  > what he enjoyed . . . "I won; he gave me $10"

- Use the words he uses . . . "finally up with the big hitters"

- When he uses an illustration, note those features *he* describes as important . . .
  "first order from P&B — took year to do — nobody suggested — sold Chief
  Engineer first"

- Take quotes verbatim . . ."teacher said, 'Harry, you're incredible'"

- Note any numbers used . . . "made $38.47 my first day"

FOURTH — Have the typist collate what the interviewee has written in SIMA Part I (pp 3-8) an
the notes you will be taking of what he says. Instruct her to leave wide margins on both sides of th
page. If you tape the interview, you can have the interview transcribed or you can listen to the tap
and amplify notes you have taken previously.

Now refer back to the second procedure, go to the next page, and start your interview.

REMEMBER! · · ·NO LEADING QUESTIONS!

Childhood
(a-1)

(a-2)

What was your role? Tell me about that.

Teen Years
(b-1)

Bird-dogging? What's involved in that?

(b-2)

NOTES   Walk through no doors which he hasn't opened.

Age 18-22
(c-1)

"Can you give me an example---an illustration?"

(c-2)

Age 22-25   Stop peeking behind the facts
(d-1)

(d-2)

Discussion of weakness is off limits.

NOTES   Remember: NO LEADING QUESTIONS!

Age 26-30
(e-1)

(e-2)

"What do you mean by the word 'coordinating'?"

Age 31-35
(f-1)

Don't summarize what he has said.

(f-2)

Keep milking until you have the details.

Age 36-40
(g-1)

(g-2)   "What did you enjoy about that?"

Age 41-45
(h-1)

              "Tell me more. Give me some details."

(h-2)

NOTES

Don't probe causation!

Age 46 and later
(i-1)

(i-2)

NOTE

Professional Motivated Abilities Pattern reports for yourself or for employees are available by contacting PMI-2, People Management Inc., 10 Station Street, Simsbury, Conn. 06070